THE COTTAGECORE WINTER

Gazing Beyond The Holidays:

Redefining The Magical Chills Of Winter

Karima Ameziani

To the winter wanderers and seekers of cozy moments,
who find joy in the serenity of snow-kissed landscapes,
and in the quiet marvels of the season,
this book is tenderly offered to you.

May its chapters kindle the fires of winter within your soul,
and encourage you to embrace the frosty enchantment in
every facet of your journey.

With warmth and appreciation,

Karima

Acknowledgment

I do not claim to be a writer;
I am simply a kindred spirit,
sharing what has brought me light,
hoping it might find those who need this help.
So please, focus on the moon I am pointing at,
not the hand that points to it.

Shared with passion and love.

TABLE OF CONTENTS

INTRODUCTION

When I woke this morning, something felt magical, and as I pulled open the curtains, the world outside revealed itself, cloaked in a shimmering blanket of snow. I gasp!

No matter how many winters I've lived through, the sight of fresh snow always manages to take my breath away, as if seeing it for the very first time.

Each delicate flake, falling from the heavens in its silent descent, felt like a whisper from the sky—a reminder that there is still magic in the world. The way the snow glistened in the pale morning light was nothing short of mesmerizing. I stood there, utterly still, as if the snow had the ability to pause time itself.

My thoughts, once swirling with the noise of everyday life, suddenly softened, absorbed into the pure quiet that only snowfall brings. It's as if the snow has a secret ability to hush the world. Scientifically, snowflakes are designed to absorb sound, softening the edges of the world's usual clamor, but it feels much deeper than that. It doesn't just silence the world outside—it silences something inside of me too. In those moments, I can hear my own heartbeat, the gentle hum of my breath, and nothing more. The physical hush mirrors an emotional one, creating a space so serene it feels sacred.

Outside, the trees, now crowned in frost, stood tall like guardians of a hidden winter realm. Every surface was touched by this icy veil, as if nature herself had laid down a soft, quilted comforter to tuck the earth in for a long rest. And as I gazed at the pristine landscape, I couldn't help but feel a deep reverence, a sense of connection with the quiet rhythms of the world around me.

In that stillness, I felt the pull to step outside, to immerse myself in this fleeting beauty. To feel the crunch of snow beneath my boots, to breathe in the crisp, cold air, and to be reminded that even in the coldest of seasons, there is warmth in the simple act of being present. Snow has a way of inviting us into its embrace, of asking us to pause, to breathe, and to see the world with new eyes.

This, my friend, was the magic of the first snowfall—a time to believe in the extraordinary, to embrace the ordinary, and to celebrate the exquisite beauty of winter's gentle touch.

Well now dear readers, or shall I say kindred spirits? Let me introduce you to "The *Cottagecore Winter*".
This book is a celebration of the art of living intentionally. In a world that sometimes feels like a whirlwind, where life can become a blur, this book is your companion to embracing the beauty of each moment in this season. Winter, with its unique teachings hidden within its cold embrace, is our guide. Let's journey together and allow the season to lead us towards a life well-lived, well-loved, and a winter season that etches itself forever in our hearts.

As in my previous seasonal books, "*The Cottagecore Winter*" is more than a seasonal celebration or guide, it has your favorite type of chapter, a complete chapter dedicated to practical steps, activity suggestions, bucket list inspiration, the season's best books, movies, songs, and mouthwatering recipes. These are the tools to fully immerse yourself in the magic of winter, to feel its essence, and to celebrate its distinctive allure.

Now, I want you to focus here dear kindred spirits, In a world that often make us rush through packed schedules, we can find ourselves sleepwalking through life, the changing seasons offer us a powerful reminder of the beauty of the present moment. They're like chapters in a grand book of life, each one with its own unique story to tell. To merely exist through these chapters without truly experiencing them is to miss out on the full richness of existence.

As we journey through the seasons, we experience life in its various forms and moods. The vibrant blossoms of spring, the sun-kissed days of summer, the crisp golden hues of autumn, and the serene beauty of winter—they all contribute to our growth and understanding of the world around us. The seasons, like wise teachers, invite us to learn from them, to be present in each moment, and to relish the unique gifts they bestow.

It's in these seasonal transitions that we find our connection with the natural world deepening. We witness the dance of life as flora and fauna adapt and evolve with the changing environment. We come to understand that we too are a part of this beautiful tapestry of existence. Our senses become attuned to the subtle shifts in the air, the scent of blooming flowers, the sound of leaves rustling, and the feel of snowflakes on our skin.

Let's dive into this journey now, this journey through "*The Cottagecore Winter.*" It's an opportunity to fully embrace the magic of winter and to savor its unique moments, for life is more than just passing through it—it's about fully living each day, each season, and finding fulfillment in the beauty that surrounds us. Let's allow the seasons to guide us, to make us feel alive, and to help us grow in harmony with nature.

Chapter I

A Winter's Enchantment

Embracing Nature's Wonderland

*In winter's silent embrace, behold,
Nature's wonderland, serene and
cold.*

*Where snowflakes dance in the crisp
air, And frosty branches glisten, oh
so fair.*

*The earth, in white, wears a
sparkling gown, A landscape of
enchantment all around.*

*With every step, a soft crunch and
creak, A symphony of stillness,
tranquil and meek.*

 As we step into this chapter, I find myself welcoming you into a world where winter is not just a season but a poetic symphony of nature's most enchanting moments. For those who may have harbored reservations about the chill in the air, let me paint for you the wonders that await.

In the heart of winter's embrace, there exists a magic that transcends the mere drop in temperature. It's a time when nature adorns itself with a crystal mantle, transforming the world into a wonderland of ethereal beauty. Each snowflake, delicate and intricate, holds within it a secret, whispering tales of resilience and grace that we, too, can embody in our own lives.

To those who have yet to uncover the allure of winter, let me be your guide to discovering the hidden treasures within this enchanting season. From the untouched serenity of snow-draped forests to the mesmerizing dance of snowflakes in the wintry breeze, there is a romance that only winter can kindle, one that ignites the soul and awakens a sense of wonder within.

Let us walk hand in hand through this snow-covered paradise, where every step leads us closer to the heart of nature. Embrace the crisp air that fills your lungs and the sight of evergreen trees frosted with snow, for it is in these moments that the true meaning of winter's embrace becomes clear. It is a reminder to slow down, to cherish the present, and to find beauty even in the coldest of moments.

In this chapter, let us unravel the mystery and magic of winter together, and may you, too, discover the enchantment that lies within the heart of nature's wintry embrace.

Dear readers, I think, Winter always, far from being a season of desolation, becomes a sanctuary for the soul, a place where we can find respite from the chaos of daily life and reconnect with the essence of our being, allowing us to emerge renewed, refreshed, and ready to embrace the beauty of the world around us.

In the grand tapestry of existence, each season is a unique thread woven delicately into the fabric of life, every season offers a unique perspective on the ever-evolving landscape of the natural world. While it may be easy to gravitate towards the warmth and vibrancy of certain seasons, it is equally essential to recognize the beauty and significance that each season brings, including the often-underappreciated allure of winter, especially after the holiday season has passed.

 Winter, with its frosty landscapes and ethereal stillness, offers a profound opportunity for introspection and contemplation, inviting us to slow down and reconnect with the quieter rhythms of life. While it may seem daunting to appreciate a season characterized by its cold and darkness, winter beckons us to find beauty in the simplicity of its stark landscapes and to cozy up inside our homes, in the intricate patterns etched by frost on windows, and in the delicate dance of snowflakes as they swirl in the wintry air. It encourages us to embrace the cozy comfort of a crackling fire, the warmth of a soft blanket, and the joy of indulging in hearty, nourishing meals that nourish both body and soul. Even for those who may not count themselves as fans of the winter season, there exists a treasure trove of delights waiting to be discovered once the holiday festivities have faded into memory.

Capturing Winter Moments

In the heart of winter's enchantment, there lies an opportunity to capture the essence of the season in all its pristine glory. The soft, diffused light that bathes the snow-covered landscapes creates an ideal setting for photography, allowing one to immortalize the serene beauty of the winter world in a series of breathtaking snapshots. You just have to learn the art of noticing, noticing magic... the way the light reflects off the icy surfaces, the delicate patterns created by frost on windows and leaves, and the intricate designs of snowflakes as they settle on various surfaces all present an endless array of subjects for the discerning photographer. Even for those who prefer the medium of painting or sketching, winter offers a wealth of inspiration, with its stark contrasts, subtle textures, and ethereal landscapes providing a rich tapestry of visual stimuli to evoke the imagination and ignite the creative spirit. Winter, far from being a monochromatic season, is a time when the world becomes a unique, different living canvas, inviting us to capture its fleeting beauty and preserve it for generations to come.

In the quiet stillness of a winter's day, the act of capturing the essence of the season becomes more than just a hobby; it becomes a form of meditation, a way of immersing oneself in the present moment, feeling most alive and finding beauty in the most unexpected of places. The delicate intricacies of a snowflake, the play of light and shadow on a frosted landscape, and the ever-changing hues of the winter sky all become a source of inspiration, encouraging us to see the world through an artist's lens and to appreciate the magic that exists in the simplest of details. As we seek to capture these fleeting moments, we are reminded of the impermanence of life and the importance of cherishing each passing season, each changing landscape, and each unique snowflake as a testament to the ephemeral beauty that surrounds us.

Winter's Calming Influence

In the gentle hush of this season, there exists a sense of calm that transcends the cold and envelops the soul in a blanket of serenity.

Amidst the quiet beauty of a snow-covered landscape, the cares of the world seem to melt away, replaced by a profound sense of contentment and gratitude for the present moment. The crisp, clean air that fills the lungs, the soft touch of snowflakes on the skin, and the sight of evergreen trees draped in a delicate veil of frost all contribute to an atmosphere of peace that is both tangible and palpable. The simple act of breathing in the cold, wintry air becomes a reminder of the importance of being present in the moment, of appreciating the beauty that surrounds us, and of finding solace in the stillness that exists within and without. Winter, becomes a sanctuary for the soul, a place where we can find respite from the chaos of daily life and reconnect with the essence of our being, allowing us to emerge renewed, refreshed, and ready to embrace the beauty of the world around us.

Connecting with Winter Nature

In each unique season, there exists a deep opportunity to connect with nature, and during winter it exists in a way that is both intimate and transformative. The tranquility of a snowy forest invites introspection and mindfulness, allowing us to find solace and peace amidst the hushed beauty of the natural world. The stillness of the air, the soft rustle of the wind through the snow-laden branches, and the occasional call of a winter bird create a symphony of serenity that is both calming and invigorating.

The simple act of taking a walk through the snow, with each step leaving a temporary impression that is soon covered by fresh flakes, becomes a metaphor that provides an ideal backdrop for cultivating a deeper connection with the natural world and discovering a sense of harmony and balance that is often elusive in the chaos of modern living.

Outdoor Activities

In the embrace of the winter wonderland, the notion of play takes on a new dimension, as the snowy terrain becomes a canvas for endless adventures and shared moments of joy. The sound of laughter rings through the air as families come together to build snow forts and create intricate snow sculptures, their hands and hearts warmed by the shared experience of playful creativity. The thrill of sledding down gentle slopes or the excitement of trying one's hand at ice fishing becomes a cherished memory that lingers long after the winter season has passed. Even the simplest of activities, such as taking a leisurely walk through the snow-covered woods (more unique and magical activity ideas in the upcoming chapters) or warming up by a crackling fire after a day of outdoor exploration, holds a special place in the heart, reminding us that winter is not just a season of cold, but a time for fostering connections, creating memories, and finding joy in the simple pleasures that life has to offer.

Winter Wildlife

Let's not forget also that in the heart of winter, the resilience 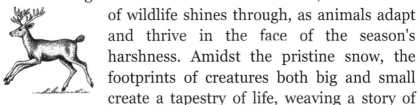 of wildlife shines through, as animals adapt and thrive in the face of the season's harshness. Amidst the pristine snow, the footprints of creatures both big and small create a tapestry of life, weaving a story of survival and endurance. From the nimble fox leaving its delicate prints on the snow to the graceful deer foraging for food beneath the frost, each animal demonstrates a remarkable ability to navigate the challenges of the season. The bird songs that pierce the wintry silence remind us that life persists even in the midst of the cold, and the squirrels that scurry to and fro gathering their winter provisions showcase a dedication to preparation and foresight. Winter, far from being a barren season, is a time when nature's resilience is on full display, a testament to the strength and adaptability of the natural world.

Inside this wilderness, a silent but vibrant community thrives, each member contributing to the delicate balance that sustains the ecosystem. The howls of wolves echo through the snow-laden trees, a reminder of the wild spirit that refuses to be tamed by the cold. The elusive hares leave behind their distinctive tracks, a testament to their ability to navigate the unforgiving terrain with grace and agility. Even the smallest of creatures, such as the tiny chickadee, find a way to survive, their cheerful chirps and playful antics serving as a reminder that even in the harshest of conditions, there is joy to be found in the simplest of moments. Winter, is a season when the resilience of wildlife inspires us to persevere and adapt, to find strength in the face of adversity, and to embrace the challenges that life presents with courage and grace.

The Beauty of Snow

 In the dance of snowflakes, there is a delicate poetry that captures the imagination. Each snowflake, with its detailed and unique design, seems to be a testament to the artistry of nature itself. Each delicate flake, a miniature work of art, delicately alights upon the earth, weaving a soft, white quilt that blankets the world in a serene hush. Settling upon the outstretched branches and tender blades of grass, they bestow upon the landscape an enchanting transformation, akin to the gentle draping of a bridal veil upon Mother Nature herself. The scene unfolds as if nature, in all her glory, has adorned herself in the purest of white gowns, casting an ethereal spell that renders the surroundings an exquisite

wonderland of pristine beauty and quiet magic. The way they catch the light, shimmering and glistening in the wintry sun, evokes a sense of awe and wonder at the delicate intricacies of the natural world.

Winter memories

 By the warmth of the crackling fireplace, I allow my mind to drift back to cherished memories of childhood winters (I invite you to do so too), each moment painted in hues of nostalgia and wonder. I remember, with vivid clarity, the joy of waking up to a world transformed by a fresh blanket of snow, the sheer delight of peering out of frost-kissed windows to behold a landscape straight out of a storybook. The tingling excitement that coursed through my veins as I bundled up in layers of wool and scarves, my breath creating ephemeral clouds in the wintry air, remains a cherished sensation, one that invoked a sense of adventure and anticipation as I ventured into the frosty embrace of the great outdoors.

I recall with fondness the thrill of crafting snowmen with rosy-cheeked friends, our laughter echoing through the stillness of the winter landscape, each snowball and each hastily assembled figure becoming a testament to our shared joy and camaraderie. The playfulness of snowball fights and the artistry of crafting intricate snow forts became a canvas for our youthful exuberance, a playground where imaginations ran wild and the boundaries of reality blurred into a world of endless possibilities. In those moments, surrounded by the laughter of friends and the shimmering embrace of snow, I felt a profound sense of belonging, as if winter itself had wrapped its comforting arms around us, embracing us in its cozy, familiar embrace.

As the day waned and the twilight cast long, blue shadows across the snow, I remember the comforting embrace of home, the aroma of hot cocoa wafting through the air, and the soft glow of lamplight casting a warm, inviting ambiance. The scent of my mother's cooking would drift from the kitchen, a tantalizing invitation that beckoned us home. The familiar aroma of simmering stews and hearty soups, the comforting scent of freshly baked bread, and the delicate sweetness of her signature hot cocoa mingled together in a symphony of flavors that filled the house with an undeniable sense of warmth and belonging. The simple act of shedding layers of winter attire and nestling into the welcoming warmth of home became a ritual of comfort and solace, a reminder that even in the coldest of moments, there existed a haven where love and warmth flourished. In the flickering candlelight and the gentle crackle of the fire, winter transformed from a season of chill to a time of cherished togetherness, where the bonds of family and the comforts of home enveloped us in a sense of security and belonging that remains etched in my heart to this day.

Chapter II

Winter Beyond the Holidays

Finding Fulfillment After The Holidays

Beyond the festive cheer and yuletide tales, In winter's quiet grace, a deeper journey unveils. Where the heart seeks solace and the soul finds reprieve, In the gentle hush of snow, we learn to believe.

In the subtle whispers of the frost-kissed air, A serenity blossoms, beyond all compare. With every breath, a moment to introspect, To find fulfillment in the stillness, this we must respect.

Beyond the merriment and the joyous chimes, Winter's embrace beckons, transcending times. It's in the quiet moments, where life finds its rhyme, Where the spirit finds solace, for now, and all time.

The Holiday's magic

 In the hearts of all who cherish the wintry season, there resides a profound love for the holidays, a fervent devotion that transcends the mere passage of time and enshrines the magic of cherished traditions. It is a time when the air itself seems to shimmer with anticipation, when the world dons its most enchanting garb, and when the laughter of loved ones mingles with the tinkling of sleigh bells and the resonant melodies of familiar carols. The holiday season, with its radiant displays of twinkling lights, the comforting aroma of freshly baked treats, and the palpable joy that infuses every street corner, casts a spell that is both timeless and deeply cherished, gifting us all with a sense of unity, wonder, and unbridled delight.

As the season unfolds, the streets become a canvas upon which the magic of the holidays is painted in hues of vibrant reds, lush greens, and iridescent golds. Houses adorned with intricate displays of twinkling lights and festive decorations come alive with an effervescent energy that draws neighbors and passersby into the shared celebration. The crisp wintry air carries with it the tantalizing scents of cinnamon and cloves, of freshly baked pies and hearty stews, inviting all who breathe it in to succumb to the irresistible allure of comfort and joy that seems to permeate every corner of the world. It is a time when the spirit of generosity flourishes, when acts of kindness and goodwill become the currency of the season, and when the joy of giving is celebrated as a timeless tradition that binds us all in the embrace of shared humanity.

In the hearts of children and adults alike, the holiday season weaves a tapestry of memories that endure far beyond the fleeting moments of revelry and merriment. It is a time for crafting cherished traditions, for kindling the fires of nostalgia that harken back to simpler times, and for basking in the glow of familial love and togetherness that is the hallmark of the season. From the laughter-filled gatherings around the hearth to the spirited exchanges of heartfelt gifts, each moment becomes a precious gem in the treasure trove of memories that we carry with us throughout our lives. It is a time when the laughter of children and the shared joy of loved ones become the melody that accompanies the dance of the season, infusing every step with a resonance that lingers long after the final notes of holiday music have faded into the wintry night.

Winter Beyond the Holidays

As the final echoes of festive melodies drifted into the wintry air, a profound stillness settled over the world, as if nature herself paused to catch her breath. The streets, once adorned with twinkling lights and bustling with the infectious energy of merrymaking, now lay bathed in a soft, ethereal glow, the remnants of joyous celebrations lingering like a tender caress upon the quietude of the wintry landscape. It was a time when the magic of the holidays still lingered in the hearts of all who had partaken in its spell, a time when the warmth of familial bonds and the shared laughter of loved ones remained as an echo of the season's revelry. And yet, it was also a time when the world seemed to exhale, releasing the jubilant energy of the festivities to reveal a deeper, more introspective essence that lay nestled within the heart of winter's embrace.

Beneath the gentle luminescence of the wintry moon, the snow-laden streets transformed into a silvery tableau of dreams. It was as if the very air hummed with the residual enchantment of the holidays, whispering secrets of wonder and joy to those willing to listen. In the midst of this hushed winter sanctuary, there existed a profound *opportunity*, a chance for *those who sought to delve into the hidden recesses of their own souls*, to unearth a fulfillment that transcended the fleeting pleasures of the festive season and found solace in the timeless beauty of the soul's yearning for deeper meaning.

The post-holiday period became a sacred threshold, a space where the echoes of laughter and the shared moments of togetherness coalesced into a symphony of memories that resonated deep within the hearts of kindred spirits. It was a time for nurturing the seeds of dreams and aspirations that had been sown amidst the laughter and camaraderie of the holiday gatherings, and for embracing the quiet fulfillment that could be found in the gentle lull that followed the frenetic energy of the festivities. Just as the earth surrendered to the restful slumber of winter, so too did weary souls find reprieve, unfurling their own stories amidst the delicate dance of frost-kissed branches and the ethereal serenade of the winter wind. It was a time for kindling the fires of passion and creativity, for savoring the moments of solitude and reflection, and for indulging in the balm of self-love that so often eludes us in the rush of everyday life. In the gentle flicker of candlelight and the aromatic embrace of steaming mugs of cocoa, there existed a sanctuary for the weary and the dreamers alike, a haven where the soul found respite and the heart found refuge in the gentle embrace of fulfillment that transcended the boundaries of time and space.

Now winter, beyond the ephemeral sparkle of the holidays, was a season that beckoned the soul to find fulfillment not in the external trappings of the world, but in the eternal wellspring of joy and contentment that flowed from within, gifting those who dared to embrace its enchantment with a timeless tale of self-discovery, inner awakening, and the eternal quest for fulfillment that transcended the boundaries of time and space. It is during these times that there is an opportunity to find solace in the simple pleasures that the season has to offer. The act of taking a walk through a snow-dusted forest, with the soft crunch of snow beneath our boots and the faint whisper of the wind through the bare trees, becomes a reminder of the delicate balance that exists within the natural world. It is a testament to the resilience of life and the ever-present beauty that can be found even in the coldest and darkest of moments. Winter, again far from being a season to endure, becomes a time to embrace the unique charms that it holds and to find appreciation in the quiet magic that unfolds when we take the time to look beyond the surface and immerse ourselves in the essence of the season.

As we navigate the remaining days of winter, we are reminded that fulfillment is not solely derived from external sources, but rather from the deep wellspring of joy and contentment that resides within each of us. It is a reminder that the essence of winter lies not in the chaos of the holidays, but in the quiet fulfillment that comes from aligning our actions with our values afterwards, nurturing our bodies and spirits, and embracing the stillness and serenity that define the season. It is a call for self-discovery and self-care that can be found when we journey beyond the hustle and bustle of the holidays and allow ourselves to fully immerse in the quiet beauty and profound fulfillment of winter.

The spirit of the season kindles a profound sense of optimism for the future, inspiring individuals to set intentions and goals that align with their aspirations and values. It serves as a beacon of light, illuminating the path forward and instilling in hearts the courage to pursue their dreams with unwavering determination. In the flickering candlelight and the merry exchange of heartfelt gifts, there exists a tangible belief in the power of hope to transcend all obstacles and to pave the way for a future brimming with possibility and potential.

And since the final days of the year are drawing near and the world prepares to turn the page, the theme of hope and renewal serves as a reminder that every ending is a gateway to a new chapter, and that every setback is an opportunity for a triumphant comeback. It encourages individuals to embrace the spirit of resilience and perseverance, to cherish the lessons learned along the way, and to step into the future with unwavering faith in the transformative power of hope. In this way, the holiday season becomes not only a time of joyous celebration, but also a testament to the enduring spirit of the human heart, a spirit that finds solace in the timeless promise of hope and renewal, and that believes, without a shadow of doubt, in the infinite potential of the human spirit to triumph over adversity and embrace the boundless possibilities of the journey ahead.

Chapter III

Cottage Comfort

Cozying Up Your Winter Retreat

In the nook of the cottage, by the hearth's warm embrace, A symphony of comfort, a haven of grace. Where flickering flames paint shadows on the walls, And the coziness within, a cherished embrace that enthralls.

With every knitted blanket and every candle's soft glow, A sanctuary of solace, where the heart learns to grow. Where the crackling fire sings tales of old, And the rustic decor weaves stories untold.

In this winter retreat, let the spirit find its ease, Where the world outside fades, and the soul finds its peace. Embraced by the cottage's warmth, in this silent retreat, We find solace and comfort, life's most tender treat.

In this chapter, I invite you dear reader to appreciate the undeniable allure in the prospect of creating a cozy sanctuary within the confines of one's winter home, as the world outside transforms into a snowy wonderland. The concept of cottage comfort transcends the mere notion of physical warmth and delves into the realms of emotional solace and spiritual nourishment. It is a state of being that beckons individuals to embrace the simple pleasures of life, to savor the delicate nuances of comfort and contentment, and to cultivate an environment that nurtures the soul as much as it warms the body.

At the heart of achieving cottage comfort lies in the art of creating a space that exudes warmth and hospitality. From the soft glow of candlelight to the gentle crackle of a wood-burning fireplace, every element within the winter retreat serves to evoke a sense of intimacy and tranquility. It is a space where cherished mementos and heirlooms find their place alongside plump cushions and sumptuous throws, each item contributing to the tapestry of comfort that envelops all who cross the threshold.

In the pursuit of cottage comfort, the winter retreat becomes a canvas upon which individuals can express their creativity and personal style. It is a space that invites self-expression, where rustic charm and modern sophistication converge to create a harmonious blend of aesthetics that reflect the unique spirit of every homemaker. Whether through the adornment of hand-knit blankets and woven tapestries or the inclusion of vintage accents and whimsical decor, every element within the retreat becomes a testament to the art of cultivating a space that is not only visually appealing but also deeply resonant with the essence of its inhabitants.

Cottage comfort embraces the ethos of slow living, encouraging individuals to embrace a pace that is in harmony with the gentle rhythm of the winter season. It is a call to revel in the simple joys of reading by the fire, of sharing heartfelt conversations over steaming mugs of cocoa, and of immersing oneself in the beauty of stillness and contemplation. It is in this state of quietude and reflection that the true essence of cottage comfort flourishes, enveloping all who dwell within its embrace in a sense of peace and serenity that transcends the boundaries of time and space.

As the winter retreat transforms into a cozy haven, it becomes a sanctuary for the soul, a space where the worries of the world are left at the doorstep and where the spirit finds solace in the gentle embrace of warmth and tranquility. It is a reminder that amidst the chaos of daily life, there exists a timeless refuge where one can find respite and renewal, and where the art of cozying up to the simple pleasures of existence becomes an ode to the enduring beauty of cottage comfort.

Within this hushed sanctuary, the outside world fades into insignificance, leaving behind only the palpable presence of love, comfort, and the enduring allure of cottage comfort that transcends the ordinary and transforms each moment into a cherished memory.

When I saw the first snowfall this morning, I knew this was not just any winter day—it was the perfect invitation to weave a tapestry of coziness throughout my home. After my invigorating stroll, where I experienced the magic of the first snow, I returned with a heart full of inspiration and excitement to create my winter retreat.

With a joyful flutter, I began to unearth my cherished winter décor, each piece a token of warmth and nostalgia. The soft, hand-knit blankets, lovingly crafted by a dear friend, beckoned for a place on the couch, while twinkling fairy lights sparkled in my mind, promising to bring a gentle glow to the dim corners of my home. I draped evergreen garlands across the mantel, their earthy scent mingling with the sweet aroma of spiced cider simmering on the stove. Every piece carried its own story, from delicate glass snowflakes to rustic wooden figurines, each finding its rightful place in the comforting embrace of my winter retreat. As I adorned the windowsills with flickering candles, the soft light flickered like tiny stars captured within the warmth of my home, inviting both reflection and reverie. This was not just decoration; it was the alchemy of the season, transforming my space into a haven where the chill of the outside world melted away, replaced by the enveloping warmth of cozy corners, the laughter of loved ones, and the magic of winter's embrace.

Creating your own winter retreat

Here are some whimsical tips on creating a winter retreat as cozy as an offered holiday vacation that lasts all season and fills your heart with merry through the long months of darkness.

Winter Natural Ornaments: Embrace the beauty of winter nature by incorporating natural ornaments like dried flowers, pinecones, evergreen branches, and woven wreaths, infusing your interiors with the rustic allure of the outdoors.

Winter colored Cozy Textiles: Layer your living spaces with plush blankets, faux fur throws, and soft area rugs to create a warm and inviting atmosphere. Opt for winter color textiles (Such as white, red, shades of blue, and pine green) that evoke a sense of comfort and coziness.

Personal Touches: Infuse your winter décor with personal touches like family winter photographs, handmade ornaments, or sentimental trinkets that evoke cherished memories and create a sense of warmth and nostalgia within your living space.

Earthy Tones: Incorporate earthy and natural color palettes such as deep greens, warm browns, and muted reds to create a cozy and inviting atmosphere. These colors can be introduced through accent pillows, wall art, or decorative vases.

Create Intimate Nooks: Design intimate corners within your home that beckon you to linger and unwind. Set up a snug reading nook by the window to read while you watch the snow storm and sip hot cocoa in your favorite winter cup, complete with a soft armchair, a fluffy winter colored blanket, and a small table for your favorite books and hot beverages.

 Remember that the best decorations are those that resonate with your personal style and create a warm and inviting atmosphere that you and your loved ones can enjoy and relax in during the winter season.

Here is a list of my favorite items to use for winter decoration:

Pinecones: Natural pinecones can be used in various ways, from table centerpieces to wreath decorations.

Evergreen Branches: Fresh or faux evergreen branches and wreaths can add a touch of greenery to your décor.

Candles: Whether real or LED, candles can provide a warm and cozy ambiance.

Holiday Lights: String lights can be hung indoors and outdoors to create a magical atmosphere. (I leave mine past the holidays till the end of winter)

Ornaments: Christmas tree ornaments can be repurposed for various decorative elements after the holidays to keep the merry warm feeling of cozy winter.

Wreaths: Hang wreaths on doors or walls for a festive touch.

Rustic Wooden Decor: Items like wooden crates, trays, and signs can add a cottagecore feel.

Knit or Crochet Items: Blankets, stockings, and pillow covers in cozy fabrics can make your space feel warm.

Seasonal Artwork: Pictures or paintings that feature winter scenes or holiday themes can add a festive touch.

Vintage Wintery Decor: Old sleds, ice skates, and other vintage winter items can be used for a charming look.

Faux Fur Throws: Plush and soft throws can create a sense of warmth and comfort.

Seasonal Tableware: Special dishes, mugs, and table linens can make your dining area feel wintery and cozy.

Seasonal Pillows: Swap out your usual throw pillows for seasonal ones with winter motifs.

Garlands: String garlands made of pine, cranberries, or even popcorn.

Snowflakes: Hang snowflake decorations or make paper snowflakes for your windows.

Berries and Twigs: Decorative branches with berries or twigs can add a rustic touch.

Vintage Sleds: Vintage sleds can be used as decorative pieces in your home or garden.

Cozy Rugs: Area rugs with warm, plush textures can make your space feel cozier.

Frosty Branches: Artificial frosted branches can add a wintry touch to your décor.

Fairy Tale Books: Display vintage or new books with winter or fairy tale themes for a cozy reading nook. (Find my winter poems book on amazon)

Faux Snow: Create a wintry scene using artificial snow or snow spray on windowsills or as a base for decorations.

Plaid Accents: Incorporate plaid blankets, table runners, or ribbons for a classic winter look.

Wintertime Potpourri: Display bowls of potpourri with scents like pine, cranberry, or cedar to fill your home with seasonal fragrance.

Chapter IV

Whispers of Snow

Embracing Winter's Delights

In the treasury of winter, a list unfurls, A trove of experiences, a map for the souls. From sleigh rides and bonfires to stargazing nights, The bucket list beckons, weaving its inviting lights.

With every checked box, an adventure to recall, A memory crafted, destined not to fall. In the wintry landscape, a journey of delight, The bucket list guides, like stars in the night.

Embrace each experience, let the spirit soar, For in these wintry moments, life finds its encore. As the bucket list unfolds, let the heart's flame burn, For in the resources of winter, there's always more to learn.

My dear reader, you finally made it to your favorite chapter! As we find ourselves nestled in the enchanting embrace of winter, there is a gentle hush that descends upon the world, bringing with it the whispers of snow that evoke a sense of wonder and magic. In this ethereal landscape, where the air is crisp and the stillness is profound, we are beckoned to embrace the delights that winter graciously bestows upon us.

In this chapter, we embark on a journey of discovery, where we delve into the essence of winter's offerings and embrace the joys that come with the season. Let us revel in the art of crafting our unique winter bucket list, a collection of extraordinary activities that allow us to savor the beauty of the season and create lasting memories that will warm our hearts for years to come. From the simple pleasures of cozying up by the fire with a beloved book to the exhilarating adventure of ice skating on a frozen pond, each activity on this list is carefully curated to celebrate the diverse tapestry of winter's delights. From family- friendly outings to cozy indoor activities, there's something for everyone to enjoy, regardless of age or preference. Our excitement for the season's arrival will grow stronger in this chapter.

 So, let's embark on this exhilarating journey, dear reader, and immerse ourselves in the wonders of the winter season. Let us embrace the crisp embrace of the frost-kissed air and the ethereal whispers of snow that beckon us to revel in the magic of the moment. With our hearts open to the joyous possibilities that await, let's venture forth into a world adorned with the enchantment of winter's delights. Together, we'll create cherished memories, share heartfelt laughter, and bask in the warmth of togetherness, as we weave our way through a tapestry of wintertime adventures that will surely leave an indelible mark on our souls. Get a pen and a steaming hot beverage, create a cozy winter ambiance that wraps us in its comforting embrace, and let's begin our exploration of the many treasures this magical season has in store for us.

Allow winter's enchantment to wrap you in its frosty embrace, captivating your heart and soul with its ethereal beauty. But first:

Your Winter To-Do List

- o Decorate your home with cozy winter-colored textures, and décor.
- o Update your wardrobe with soft layers and wintery colored clothes.
- o Curate a list of exhilarating winter activities, and outings to prepare for.
- o Indulge in the flavors of the season with soul-warming culinary delights and comforting hot beverages.
- o Unleash your creativity with winter-inspired DIY projects.
- o Read winter themed books, and literature that evoke the enchantment of the season.
- o Watch classic winter-themed movies and series that capture the magic of this frost-kissed season.

As we welcome winter by preparing our hearts and homes to embrace the season's cozy charm. With the frosty landscape as our muse, we adorn our living spaces with plush blankets, aromatic candles, and accents that evoke the serene beauty of the winter wonderland. The atmosphere transforms into a haven of warmth, where the spirit of winter finds solace and comfort.

Updating our wardrobe becomes a delightful ritual, as we layer up in soft knits, woolen scarves, and snug hats, ready to brave the chilly days with grace and elegance. There's a certain thrill in the process, as we embrace the art of winter dressing, curating a wardrobe that embodies the essence of the season's palette and textures.

As the wintry chill sets in, our wardrobes undergo a magical transition, bidding adieu to the light fabrics of autumn and welcoming the cozy layers and rich tones that define winter fashion. It's akin to unearthing a treasure trove of soft sweaters, warm scarves, and stylish outerwear, each piece whispering tales of comfort and sophistication that epitomize the essence of the season.

Refreshing Your Winter Wardrobe

Rediscover Your Seasonal Favorites

Begin by unpacking your treasured winter garments from storage. Revel in the nostalgia as you reunite with your beloved coats, sweaters, and scarves from winters past. Each piece carries with it the essence of cherished memories and snug comfort from bygone snowy days.

Embrace Winter's Cool Palette

Winter ushers in a serene and cool-toned color palette, featuring shades like deep navy, forest green, rich burgundy, and icy gray. Embrace these hues as you curate your winter wardrobe, infusing it with the tranquil tones that mirror the season's essence.

Indulge in Cozy Knitwear Layers

Revel in the joy of layering, a quintessential aspect of winter fashion. Pair your coziest sweaters with thermal tops or turtlenecks, creating ensembles that exude both warmth and sophistication on frosty days.

Wrap Yourself in Cozy Scarves

Beyond their practicality, scarves serve as stylish accents during the winter months. Invest in an array of scarves boasting different textures and patterns, effortlessly elevating your outfits with a touch of opulence and comfort.

Adorn with Elegant Headwear

From timeless wool fedoras to snug beanies, winter hats are the ultimate statement pieces for your seasonal ensemble. Experiment with various hat styles to add a touch of elegance and personality to your winter look.

Mix and Match with Flair

Unleash your creativity by blending and combining your winter pieces. Experiment with diverse textures, prints, and colors to craft distinctive and captivating outfits that reflect your individuality and winter style.

Add Personal Flourishes

Infuse your wardrobe with personal touches that reflect your unique taste. Consider incorporating wintry-themed brooches, vintage accessories, or seasonal statement jewelry to showcase your love for the season.

 As you step out adorned in your winter finery, you embody the essence of the season with a grace and style as mesmerizing as the falling snow. Let the joy of dressing up in winter's finest be your daily celebration of the enchanting and serene time of the year.

Making Your Bucket List

As the first snowflake graces our palms, we welcome the arrival of winter with a spark of excitement in our souls. Together, we'll compile a list of winter activities and cozy pastimes that fill us with anticipation. We'll wander through snow-kissed landscapes, where every tree and rooftop wears a devine white coat, and our breath mingles with the frosty air, creating an enchanting winter symphony.

Now, my dear reader, take a moment to craft your own list on the following page, allowing your thoughts to dance freely amidst the winter's wonder. Let your pen capture the unique sensations, cherished memories, and the elements that make winter a season of magic for you. For inspiration, the next section unfolds, where the essence of winter comes alive in all its breathtaking splendor. So, whether you choose to lose yourself in introspection or seek a spark from the upcoming inspiration, let us join hands and immerse ourselves in the enchanting embrace of winter.

Winter Bucket List

☐
☐
☐
☐
☐
☐
☐
☐
☐
☐
☐
☐
☐
☐
☐
☐
☐
☐
☐
☐
☐
☐
☐
☐
☐
☐
☐

Winter Bucket List Inspiration

- Create a winter-themed playlist (check out music suggestions in the upcoming chapter)
- switch your wardrobe.
- Make a winter vision board.
- collect snowflakes on your gloves during a winter hike.
- Master the art of baking gingerbread cookies, or hearty stews to relish the flavors of the season.
- Indulge your senses with winter treats like peppermint hot chocolate, spiced apple tarts, and warm cinnamon rolls.
- Dive into your favorite winter novel snuggled up by a crackling fireplace.
- Craft nourishing soups like creamy potato soup or classic chicken noodle soup.
- Engage in knitting or crocheting to fashion cozy blankets, scarves, and mittens to keep the chill at bay.
- Plan visits to local holiday markets and snowy wonderlands for a delightful winter experience.
- Attend winter festivals, holiday concerts, and cultural events in your area to celebrate the spirit of the season.
- Embark on winter-themed DIY projects (check out DIY suggestions in the upcoming chapter)

- Capture the breathtaking beauty of winter landscapes with a brush and canvas (Or your camera).
- Host a winter movie marathon with classic snowy tales and heartwarming stories (movie recommendations to follow).
- Spend a day at a quaint café, sipping a hot beverage while watching the snowfall outside.
- Visit a winter wonderland and revel in the serene beauty of snowy landscapes.
- Dress appropriately and arrange a cozy picnic in the snow, complete with warm blankets and savory winter delights.
- Capture the winter magic with a photoshoot in a snow-covered park.
- Embrace the childlike joy of building snowmen and making snow angels on a crisp winter day.
- Go ice skating on a frozen lake or at a local ice rink, savoring the exhilaration of gliding on ice. (be safe)
- Plan a weekend getaway to a charming cabin nestled amidst a snow-laden forest.
- Read soul-stirring winter poetry from renowned authors.
- Host a festive gathering with loved ones, toasting marshmallows, and sharing heartwarming tales.
- Explore the art of winter photography, capturing the ethereal landscapes and fleeting moments of the season's enchantment.
- Go for a horse ride in a snowy landscape park or meadow.

o Have a winter vibes day where all what you do is winter themed.

Capturing Winter Details of Magic

These are some photography and painting ideas to capture the essence of winter:

Frosty Landscapes: Capture the intricate details of frost-covered landscapes, showcasing the delicate patterns formed by frost on leaves, branches, and grass.

Snowy Sceneries: Capture the serene beauty of snow-covered landscapes, from untouched fields to snow-laden trees and rooftops. Experiment with different angles and perspectives to convey the tranquility and purity of winter.

Icy Details: Zoom in on the intricate details of icy surfaces, such as frozen water droplets, icicles hanging from rooftops, or frost formations on windows. Highlight the play of light on these icy textures to add depth and dimension to your composition.

Winter Wildlife: Capture the resilience of wildlife during the winter season. Photograph or paint animals such as birds, squirrels, or deer amidst snowy backdrops, highlighting their adaptations to the cold weather.

Winter Activities: Document the joy and excitement of winter activities such as ice skating, skiing, or sledding. Capture the movement, energy, and exhilaration of these activities, showcasing the human connection with the winter environment.

Indoor Coziness: Capture the warmth and comfort of indoor spaces during winter. Photograph or paint cozy corners, roaring fireplaces, or people wrapped in blankets, showcasing the intimacy and tranquility of indoor living during the colder months.

Winter Sunsets and Sunrises: Capture the breathtaking colors and hues of winter sunsets and sunrises. Experiment with silhouettes, shadows, and reflections to convey the magical and ephemeral nature of these celestial displays.

Frozen Water Bodies: Photograph or paint frozen lakes, rivers, or waterfalls, capturing the stillness and serenity of these icy landscapes. Focus on the contrast between the frozen water and the surrounding elements to create a striking visual narrative.

Winter Textures: Zoom in on various winter textures, such as snow-covered tree bark, frozen berries, or frosted pine needles. Showcase the intricate details and unique patterns that emerge during the winter season, emphasizing the tactile and visual aspects of these elements.

Winter Traditions: Capture the essence of winter traditions and celebrations, such as holiday decorations, family gatherings, or community events. Document the joy, warmth, and togetherness that define these festive moments, portraying the cultural significance of winter customs.

Experiment with these ideas to encapsulate the enchanting and transformative qualities of winter, allowing your photography or artwork to reflect the distinctive charm and allure of the season.

Chapter V

Resources for the Winter Journey

Softly, the snow whispers tales untold, A dance of delicate flakes, a sight to behold. In each icy crystal, a world in miniature, A wonderland unfolds, pure and sure.

With every step, the snow crunches and sings, A melody of winter, on gossamer wings. Embracing the chill, the world becomes still, As whispers of snow, the heart does fill.

In this wintry embrace, let the spirit take flight, In the arms of the season, find pure delight. For in each snowflake's descent, a moment to treasure, Embracing winter's whispers, an experience beyond measure.

As I sat by the window, watching the delicate snowflakes dance and twirl outside, I felt a gentle urge to capture the magic unfolding before me. Each flake fell softly, creating a serene landscape that begged to be admired. I grabbed a pen and paper, ready to write about the treasures I wanted to explore during this enchanting winter journey.

In that moment, I was struck by the idea of creating a cozy atmosphere, both within and around me. I envisioned curling up with captivating books that painted vivid portraits of snowy landscapes and heartwarming tales. I recalled how, in past winters, I lost myself in stories that whisked me away to places where laughter echoed around roaring fires and friends gathered to share the warmth of companionship. With the snow continuing to fall, I turned my thoughts to music, imagining a playlist filled with soft, melodic tunes that would serenade me as I embraced the quiet beauty of the season. There's something about winter melodies that brings a sense of calm, gently urging me to slow down and savor the stillness outside.

As the afternoon light began to fade, I thought about the heartwarming films that transport me to cozy retreats. Those stories always seemed to capture the essence of winter—the joy of simple pleasures, the comfort of good company, and the magic that happens when snow blankets the world. I could already feel the warmth of those films wrapping around me like a beloved blanket on a chilly evening. I envisioned delightful DIY projects to infuse my home with the spirit of the season. Gathering pinecones, twinkling lights, and fragrant spices felt like the perfect way to bring the outside in, transforming my space into a cozy retreat that echoed the beauty of the winter wonderland just beyond my window.

In this chapter, dear kindred spirit we unveil a trove of resources that will accompany us on our enchanting winter journey. From captivating books that paint vivid portraits of snowy landscapes to melodic tunes that serenade us with the whispers of the season, from heartwarming movies that transport us to cozy winter retreats to delightful DIY projects that infuse our homes with the spirit of the season—each recommendation is a cherished gem meant to enrich our experience and kindle the flame of winter's delight within our hearts. So, let us wander through these offerings, embracing the essence of winter's enchantment and allowing ourselves to be swept away by the allure of this breathtaking season.

Winter-themed books, music, and movies serve as more than just entertainment; they reflect the profound connections between art and the human experience. Just as winter encompasses moments of quiet introspection, these cultural expressions offer a bridge to our own emotions, memories, and contemplations. As the poet William Blake once eloquently observed, "In seed-time learn, in harvest teach, in winter enjoy." Through the lens of winter narratives, we find solace in shared experiences, understanding the complexities of human relationships, resilience, and the beauty of the natural world.

Winter-themed literature often delves into themes of self-discovery, resilience in the face of adversity, and the transformative power of reflection. As we immerse ourselves in these narratives, we gain insights into our own journey, finding parallels between the characters' challenges and our personal growth. Echoing the words of George R.R. Martin, "Winter is coming," these stories remind us of the need to prepare for life's challenges and embrace the strength within us during the colder seasons.

 Winter-inspired melodies and harmonies evoke emotions of nostalgia, hope, and tranquility, encouraging us to embrace the seasonal introspection and find comfort in the beauty of stillness and contemplation. As the poet John Steinbeck once mused, "What good is the warmth of summer, without the cold of winter to give it sweetness?" Winter-themed movies, with their portrayal of human connections amidst the backdrop of snow-covered landscapes, remind us of the importance of relationships, love, and the warmth of companionship during colder seasons. These films often highlight the significance of cherished moments, familial bonds, and the resilience of the human spirit, echoing the sentiment of Edith Sitwell, who wrote, "Winter is the time for comfort, for good food and warmth, for the touch of a friendly hand and for a talk beside the fire: it is the time for home."

By engaging with winter-themed cultural expressions, we connect with the profound truths and experiences that define the human condition, allowing us to appreciate the beauty of the season not just as a backdrop, but as a reflection of our own inner landscapes and the relationships that shape our lives. In this way, winter-themed arts serve as a poignant reminder of the shared human experience and the enduring resilience of the human spirit in the face of life's challenges and changes.

1. The Joys of Winter DIYs

Amidst the wintry enchantment that surrounds us, let us indulge in the adventure of creativity through delightful DIY projects that celebrate the magic of the season. These easy and elegant winter DIYs, crafted from natural elements and everyday household items, bring forth the essence of the season in the most charming and unique ways that we can enjoy making with our loved ones or just as a relaxing activity.

Here's a list of heartwarming and accessible DIYs for you to try, infusing your space with the rustic allure and cozy charm of the winter wonderland:

Snowflake Window Clings

Create delicate snowflake window clings using white glue and wax paper. Once dry, gently peel the snowflakes off and adorn your windows with these intricate winter wonders.

Citrus Winter Garland

Slice oranges, lemons, and grapefruits, and dry them in the oven. String the dried slices together with twine or ribbon to fashion a stunning and aromatic winter garland for your cozy abode.

Cinnamon Stick Ornaments

Bundle cinnamon sticks together with twine or ribbon to form adorable rustic ornaments. Hang them on your Christmas tree or use them as fragrant décor accents throughout your home.

Winter Wonderland Mason Jar Luminary

Fill a mason jar with Epsom salt and place a tea light candle inside for a mesmerizing snowy glow. Adorn the jar with twigs, pinecones, and faux berries for an enchanting winter centerpiece.

Homemade Pine Scented Candles

Melt down old candles and add pine essential oil for an invigorating wintry aroma. Pour the wax into small jars and adorn them with winter-inspired decorations for a personalized touch of seasonal warmth.

Frosted Pinecone Wreath

Collect pinecones and apply white paint to the edges for a frost-kissed effect. Arrange them in a circular pattern on a foam wreath base, interweaving with faux winter berries and leaves for a stunning and welcoming winter wreath.

Winter Terrarium

Construct a miniature winter wonderland in a glass terrarium using faux snow, small figurines, and tiny pine trees. Add a touch of whimsy and magic to your living space with this captivating winter display.

Winter Book Page Bookmark

Repurpose old book pages into charming winter-themed bookmarks by cutting them into snowflake or pine tree shapes. Add a touch of sparkle with a dusting of glitter or a simple ribbon for an elegant finish.

Winter Scented Sachets

Fill small fabric pouches with dried lavender, pine needles, and cinnamon sticks, tying them with a decorative string. Tuck these scented sachets into your drawers or hang them in your closet to infuse your wardrobe with the comforting scents of winter.

Snowy Pinecone Place Cards

Spray-paint pinecones white and attach small name cards for a charming and rustic addition to your winter table setting. Use them as place cards for your intimate gatherings or festive dinners.

Hand-Knit Coasters

Pick up some chunky yarn and knitting needles to create cozy hand-knit coasters, perfect for keeping your mugs and glasses warm and your tabletops protected during the chilly winter months.

These delightful winter DIYs, inspired by the natural elements and warmth of the season, will not only infuse your home with charm but also bring a sense of joy and creativity to your winter days. Enjoy the process and revel in the cozy beauty of the season!

II. Enchanting Lists:
Movies, Books, and Music

Whimsical Winter Movies

- "The Holiday" - A heartwarming tale of love and friendship set amidst the enchanting backdrop of the winter holidays.

- "Little Women" - A classic story that captures the essence of family bonds and the resilience of the human spirit, beautifully set in a wintry landscape.

- "The Chronicles of Narnia: The Lion, the Witch, and the Wardrobe" - A captivating fantasy film that transports viewers to a whimsical winter wonderland filled with adventure and courage.

- "Winter's Bone" - A gripping drama that follows the determined journey of a young woman as she navigates the harsh realities of rural life in the Ozark Mountains, highlighting the resilience of the human spirit in the face of adversity.

- "Frozen River" - A compelling narrative that explores the struggles of two women drawn into the world of smuggling along the frozen St. Lawrence River, emphasizing the complexities of survival and sacrifice.

- "The Revenant" - A visually stunning and intense survival epic that immerses viewers in the harrowing tale of a fur trapper's quest for vengeance in the unforgiving wilderness of the American frontier.

- "The Grand Budapest Hotel" - A whimsical and visually captivating film that unfolds the adventures of a legendary hotel concierge and his loyal lobby boy, set against the backdrop of a snowy and enchanting European landscape.

- "Silver Skates" - A classic Dutch tale set in wintry Amsterdam, following the adventures of Hans and Gretel as they navigate a story of love, adventure, and the thrill of ice-skating on frozen canals.

- "Fargo" - A darkly comedic crime series that interweaves intriguing characters and complex narratives, portraying the chilling and often bizarre events that unfold in the wintry setting of Minnesota and the surrounding Midwest.

- "Twin Peaks" - A surreal and mysterious series that delves into the enigmatic events surrounding a small town's secrets, evoking an eerie and captivating atmosphere, enhanced by the haunting beauty of the Pacific Northwest.

- "Everwood" - A poignant family drama series that follows a renowned neurosurgeon as he relocates his family to a small Colorado town, emphasizing the beauty of human connections and the challenges of embracing a new life in a picturesque winter landscape.

- "North and South" - A period drama miniseries that follows the story of a young woman's journey from the idyllic south of England to the industrial north during the 19th century. The series beautifully depicts the stark contrast between the bustling northern industrial towns and the tranquil winter landscapes of the countryside.

- "Jane Eyre" is a timeless period drama that incorporates wintry elements to evoke a sense of atmospheric beauty and emotional depth. The wintry setting in various adaptations of the story often accentuates the characters' internal struggles and the challenges they face.

- "Poldark": Set in the rugged landscapes of Cornwall, England, "Poldark" is a historical drama series that weaves a captivating tale of love, betrayal, and resilience. With its breathtaking scenery and compelling narrative, the show offers a cozy and immersive viewing experience, perfect for wintertime indulgence.

Whimsical Winter Books

- o "The Snow Child" by Eowyn Ivey - A poignant narrative that weaves the magic of a snow child into the lives of a childless couple in the Alaskan wilderness.

- o "Winter Garden" by Kristin Hannah - A captivating story of family bonds, resilience, and the healing power of love, set against the backdrop of a Russian fairy tale.

- o "Ethan Frome" by Edith Wharton - A timeless classic that delves into the complexities of human relationships and the challenges of life in a harsh New England winter.

- o "A Christmas Carol" by Charles Dickens - A beloved holiday tale that embodies the spirit of redemption and compassion, unfolding in the wintry streets of Victorian London.

- o "The Bear and the Nightingale" by Katherine Arden - An enchanting blend of fantasy and folklore that transports readers to the wintry forests of medieval Russia, filled with magic and mystery.

- o "The Wolves of Winter" by Tyrell Johnson - An exhilarating post-apocalyptic tale that unfolds in the chilling landscapes of a frozen Yukon, where a young woman must navigate the harsh winter terrain and face the challenges of survival amidst the remnants of a world ravaged by disease and disaster.

- o "The Great Alone" by Kristin Hannah - Set in the 1970s, this gripping novel tells the story of a family's journey to the Alaskan wilderness, where they encounter the untamed beauty of winter and must confront both the dangers of the natural world and the complexities of human relationships.

o "The Starless Sea" by Erin Morgenstern - A captivating fantasy novel that takes readers on a wondrous journey through a magical underground library, brimming with enchanting tales and mysterious adventures that evoke the timeless allure of winter nights.

o "One Day in December" by Josie Silver - A heartwarming contemporary romance that unfolds over a decade, tracing the interconnected lives of two individuals who experience the magic of love at first sight on a snowy December day, capturing the essence of winter romance and heartfelt connections.

o "Winter Street" by Elin Hilderbrand - The first installment of a captivating series set in Nantucket, this novel follows the lives of the Quinn family as they navigate personal challenges, family dynamics, and unexpected twists during a charming and eventful winter holiday season.

Whimsical Winter Music

- "Winter Song" by The Head and the Heart
- "Northern Wind" by City and Colour
- "Winter White" by A Fine Frenzy
- "Stubborn Love" by The Lumineers
- "Winter Winds" by Mumford & Sons
- "Falling Snow" by Agnes Obel
- "White Winter Hymnal" by Fleet Foxes
- "To Build a Home" by The Cinematic Orchestra
- "Holocene" by Bon Iver
- "Woods" by Hollow Coves
- "Winter Solstice" by Cold Weather Company
- "Michigan" by The Milk Carton Kids
- "Winter Song" by Sara Bareilles and Ingrid Michaelson
- "Follow the Sun" by Xavier Rudd
- "Woods" by Gregory Alan Isakov
- "Winter" by Joshua Radin
- "Ghosts" by James Vincent McMorrow
- "Rivers and Roads" by The Head and the Heart

- o   "Winter Bones" by Stars and Rabbit

- o   "Aurora Borealis" by Beta Radio

- o   "Frozen Pines" by Lord Huron

- o   "Butterflies In Love" by Sir Cubworth

- o   Winter ASMR Ambience videos on YouTube

These enchanting indie folk melodies evoke the nostalgia and serenity of a cottagecore winter, enveloping listeners in the soothing embrace of acoustic melodies and poetic lyrics. Don't forget to add to this list any songs you hold dear or that evokes memories and winter feels.

Chapter VI

Sips and Savories

The Taste of Winter's Warmth

In the simmering pot, a tale of winter brews, A symphony of flavors, a delightful muse. From mulled spices to savory stews, Winter's warmth resides in each hearty chew.

With every sip of cocoa, a moment to savor, A hug from within, a delightful favor. In the aroma of spices, a dance of the senses, The taste of winter's warmth, a gift that commences.

Let the recipes unfold, like chapters of delight, In the taste of winter's embrace, find pure respite. For in every savory bite, and in every sip, The essence of winter's comfort finds a cherished grip.

As I was making dinner on the first day of winter, a wave of nostalgia washed over me, drawing me back to the cherished moments spent in the kitchen with my grandmother and mother. I could almost hear my grandmother's gentle voice, guiding me through the delicate dance of flavors, her hands expertly mixing spices with the ease of a well-practiced chef. I recalled those snowy evenings when the world outside was blanketed in white, and we would gather around the stove, our cheeks rosy from the cold. Together, we would craft warm, comforting soups, the kind that felt like a hug in a bowl. Each ingredient was carefully chosen, from vibrant carrots to earthy potatoes, each slice and chop infused with love and warmth. I remembered how my mother would always insist on adding a pinch of this and a dash of that, her secret touch turning a simple stew into a feast that brought the family together.

As I stirred the pot before me, I couldn't help but smile at the memories swirling around me, mingling with the fragrant spices of winter—cinnamon, nutmeg, and cloves. I could picture my grandmother's well-worn recipe book, its pages dog-eared and stained with the remnants of countless meals shared. Those recipes were more than just instructions; they were a connection to our past, a lineage of flavors that carried the essence of our family history.

The warmth of the stove enveloped me, inviting me to create my own moments, to weave the same tapestry of flavors that had once filled our home. I decided to prepare a creamy butternut squash soup, its golden hue reminiscent of the sun peeking through the winter clouds. As I blended the squash until velvety smooth, I added a swirl of cream, allowing its richness to dance with the spices, creating a symphony of taste that whispered of comfort and joy.

With every spoonful, I felt the spirit of my grandmother and mother beside me, guiding my hands and igniting my senses. It was in this act of cooking that I discovered the true essence of winter's warmth—not just in the flavors that filled my home, but in the stories and love that came alive through each recipe.

As I ladled the soup into my bowl, I thought of the gatherings that would soon follow, the laughter and conversations that would fill the air. Winter was not just a season of cold; it was an invitation to embrace togetherness, to create moments that would be savored long after the last bite was gone. I poured myself a steaming mug of spiced cocoa, letting its rich aroma envelop me, and took a moment to breathe in the cozy atmosphere I had created.

With every sip, I was reminded that these winter flavors, steeped in memories and tradition, would continue to nurture not only my body but also my soul, transforming my home into a sanctuary of warmth and love as the snow fell gently outside.

Ah, my dear reader, join me in savoring the delightful flavors that define the essence of winter. In this chapter, we will uncover the secrets to crafting tantalizing sips and savory delicacies that embody the very spirit of the season. Imagine yourself cozied up by the crackling fire, cradling a steaming mug of spiced cocoa that awakens your senses with its rich, aromatic bliss. Envision the comforting aroma of a hearty stew simmering on the stove, promising a feast that warms not just the body, but the soul.

Discover the joy of relishing homemade soups, brimming with the season's vibrant vegetables, mirroring the colorful tapestry of the wintry landscape just beyond your window. Delight in the art of baking fresh bread, its golden crust and tender, warm interior offering solace with every slice. As you savor each spoonful and revel in each mouthwatering bite, let the flavors of winter's bounty remind you of the abundance and beauty that this season bestows upon us.

Together, let's unlock the recipes that bring to life the very essence of winter, infusing our homes with the fragrant spices of cinnamon, nutmeg, and cloves. From the aromatic allure of mulled cider to the buttery comfort of roasted vegetables, we will delve into the culinary magic that unites friends and family in the cozy embrace of the cottagecore winter. So, my dear reader, prepare to awaken your taste buds and ignite your senses with the rich and soulful flavors that this season graciously offers.

These are 10 cozy winter recipes that will fill your home with warmth and your heart with delight:

Creamy Chicken and Wild Rice Soup

Ingredients:
- 2 cups cooked chicken, shredded or diced
- 1 cup wild rice, uncooked
- 2 carrots, peeled and diced
- 2 celery stalks, diced
- 1 onion, finely chopped
- 3 cloves garlic, minced
- 1 tsp dried thyme
- 1 bay leaf
- 6 cups chicken broth
- 1 cup heavy cream
- ¼ cup all-purpose flour
- 3 tbsp butter
- Salt and pepper, to taste

Instructions:
- Sauté onion, carrots, and celery in butter until softened.
- Add garlic, thyme, and bay leaf; stir for 1-2 minutes.
- Stir in flour, then gradually whisk in chicken broth.
- Add wild rice and simmer for 40-45 minutes, until rice is cooked.
- Stir in chicken and heavy cream, simmer for 5-10 minutes.
- Season with salt and pepper. Remove bay leaf and serve!

Roasted Root Vegetables with Herbs

Ingredients:

- 3 carrots, peeled and chopped
- 3 parsnips, peeled and chopped
- 2 sweet potatoes, peeled and chopped
- 2 tbsp olive oil
- 1 tbsp fresh rosemary, chopped
- 1 tbsp fresh thyme, chopped
- Salt and pepper, to taste

Instructions:

- Toss the carrots, parsnips, and sweet potatoes with olive oil, rosemary, and thyme.
- Roast on a baking sheet at 400°F (200°C) for 25-30 minutes, or until tender and caramelized.
- Season with salt and pepper before serving.

Beef and Mushroom Stew

Ingredients:

- 1 ½ lbs stew beef, cubed
- 8 oz mushrooms, sliced
- 1 onion, chopped
- 3 cloves garlic, minced
- 3 cups beef broth
- 1 cup red wine
- 2 tbsp tomato paste
- 1 tbsp Worcestershire sauce
- 1 tsp dried thyme
- 1 bay leaf
- Salt and pepper, to taste

Instructions:

- Sear beef in a large pot until browned on all sides, then remove.

- Sauté onion, add garlic and mushrooms, cooking for 3-4 minutes.

- Stir in tomato paste and cook for 1 minute.

- Add wine, beef broth, and Worcestershire sauce. Return beef to the pot.

- Add thyme and bay leaf, then simmer for 1 ½ to 2 hours, or until beef is tender.

- Season with salt and pepper before serving.

Maple Pecan Snack Mix

Ingredients:

- 1 cup pecans
- 2 cups pretzels
- ½ cup dried cranberries
- ¼ cup maple syrup
- 2 tbsp butter
- ½ tsp cinnamon
- Pinch of salt

Instructions:

- Toast pecans in a skillet over medium heat until fragrant.
- Add pretzels and dried cranberries, stirring to combine.
- In a separate saucepan, melt butter, then stir in maple syrup, cinnamon, and a pinch of salt.
- Drizzle the maple mixture over the pecans, pretzels, and cranberries, tossing to coat.
- Let cool and enjoy this sweet and savory snack!

Cranberry - Orange Scones

Ingredients:

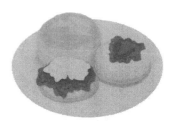

- 2 cups flour
- ¼ cup sugar
- 1 tbsp baking powder
- ½ tsp salt
- ½ cup cold butter, cubed
- ½ cup dried cranberries
- 1 tbsp orange zest
- ½ cup milk
- 1 egg (for egg wash)

Instructions:

- **Mix dry ingredients**: In a bowl, combine flour, sugar, baking powder, and salt.
- **Cut in butter**: Add cold butter and use a pastry cutter or fork to blend until the mixture is crumbly.
- **Stir in cranberries and orange zest.**
- **Add milk**: Gradually pour in the milk, stirring until a dough forms.
- **Shape into scones**: On a floured surface, shape the dough into a circle and cut into wedges.
- **Brush with egg wash** and bake at 400°F (200°C) for 15-20 minutes, or until golden brown.
- **Serve** warm!

Maple Glazed Roasted Vegetables

Ingredients:

- 2 cups Brussels sprouts, halved
- 2 cups butternut squash, cubed
- 2 tbsp olive oil
- 2 tbsp maple syrup
- Salt and pepper, to taste

Instructions:

- **Toss vegetables** with olive oil and spread on a baking sheet.
- **Roast** at 400°F (200°C) for 20-25 minutes, until almost tender.
- **Drizzle with maple syrup** and roast for another 5-10 minutes until caramelized.
- **Season** with salt and pepper before serving.

Winter Berry Pie

Ingredients:

- 4 cups mixed berries
(raspberries, blueberries,
blackberries)
- ¾ cup sugar
- 1 tbsp lemon juice
- 2 tbsp cornstarch
- 1 double pie crust (top and bottom)

Instructions:

- **Mix berries** with sugar, lemon juice, and cornstarch in a
bowl.
- **Fill the pie crust** with the berry mixture, then cover with
the second crust.
- **Bake** at 375°F (190°C) for 45-50 minutes, or until the
filling is bubbling and the crust is golden brown.
- **Cool** before serving. Enjoy!

Cranberry-Pecan Bread

Ingredients:

- 2 cups all-purpose flour
- 1 tsp baking powder
- ½ tsp baking soda
- ¼ tsp salt
- 1 cup sugar
- 1 tbsp orange zest
- ½ cup orange juice
- ½ cup butter, softened
- 2 eggs
- 1 cup cranberries
- ½ cup chopped pecans

Instructions:

- **Mix dry ingredients**: In a bowl, combine flour, baking powder, baking soda, and salt.
- **Beat sugar, orange zest, and butter** until light and fluffy. Add eggs one at a time, beating well after each addition.
- **Stir in dry ingredients** and orange juice alternately until well combined.
- **Fold in cranberries and pecans**.
- **Bake** in a greased loaf pan at 350°F (175°C) for 50-60 minutes, or until a toothpick inserted comes out clean.
- **Cool** before slicing and serving.

Winter Vegetable Stew

Ingredients:

- 3 cups assorted winter vegetables (carrots, parsnips, potatoes), chopped
- 1 onion, chopped
- 3 cloves garlic, minced
- 4 cups vegetable broth
- 1 can (14 oz) diced tomatoes
- 1 tsp dried thyme
- 1 tsp dried rosemary
- 1 bay leaf
- Salt and pepper, to taste

Instructions:

- **Sauté onions and garlic** in a large pot over medium heat until softened.
- **Add vegetables** and cook for 5-7 minutes until slightly softened.
- **Pour in broth** and add diced tomatoes, thyme, rosemary, and the bay leaf.
- **Simmer** for 25-30 minutes, or until vegetables are tender.
- **Season** with salt and pepper, and serve warm.

Cinnamon-Sugar Snowflake Cookies

Ingredients:

- 2 ¾ cups all-purpose flour
- 1 tsp baking powder
- ¼ tsp salt
- 1 cup unsalted butter, softened
- 1 cup granulated sugar
- 2 eggs
- 1 tsp vanilla extract
- 1 tsp ground cinnamon
- Powdered sugar (for dusting)

Instructions:

- **Whisk flour, baking powder, and salt** in a bowl.
- In a separate bowl, **beat butter and sugar** until light and fluffy. Add eggs and vanilla.
- **Gradually add the flour mixture**, mixing until combined.
- **Roll out the dough** on a floured surface and cut into snowflake shapes.
- **Sprinkle with cinnamon-sugar** mixture and bake at 350°F (175°C) for 8-10 minutes, or until golden.
- **Dust with powdered sugar** once cooled, and enjoy!

Cozy Sips of Winter Magic

 Hot beverages in winter serve as more than just a means of staying warm. They offer a comforting respite from the cold, providing a cozy and familiar sensation that soothes the body and soul. Sipping on a steaming cup of tea, hot chocolate, or spiced cider creates a moment of tranquility, allowing one to pause and appreciate the simple pleasures of life. Additionally, the warmth of these drinks can help alleviate the winter chill, promoting a sense of relaxation and well-being. As the steam rises from the cup and the fragrant aroma fills the air, these beverages not only warm the body but also provide a sense of comfort and nourishment during the colder months. Enjoying these hot drinks can become a cherished winter ritual, fostering a sense of connection and contentment during the season.

Here are five cozy teas and hot beverages perfect for the winter season:

Spiced Chai Tea: Brew black tea with warming spices like cinnamon, cardamom, cloves, and ginger. Add a touch of milk and sweeten with honey for a comforting and aromatic winter beverage.

Peppermint Hot Chocolate: Indulge in a rich and creamy hot chocolate infused with the cool, refreshing flavor of peppermint. Top it with whipped cream and crushed candy canes for an extra festive touch.

Mulled Apple Cider: Simmer apple cider with a blend of winter spices such as cinnamon sticks, cloves, and star anise. Add slices of fresh orange for a citrusy twist. Enjoy the cozy fragrance and warm flavors of this classic winter drink.

Vanilla Rooibos Latte: Brew rooibos tea and combine it with frothy steamed milk and a hint of vanilla syrup. Sprinkle some cinnamon on top for a fragrant and soothing beverage that's perfect for chilly winter evenings.

Ginger Turmeric Tea: Steep fresh ginger and turmeric in hot water, and add a squeeze of lemon and a drizzle of honey for a naturally soothing and immune-boosting tea that's perfect for keeping warm during the winter months.

Chapter VII

A Year-Round Embrace

Cottagecore's Promise

In the heart of the cottage, whispers unfold, A promise of winter, a tale yet untold. Where nature's embrace and simplicity entwine, Cottagecore's allure, forever divine.

Through each changing season, its essence remains, A rustic haven, where the soul entertains. In the warmth of its hearth, a solace it brings, Cottagecore's winter promise, a melody that sings.

Let's cherish its values, in every step we take, For in this year-round embrace, we find solace and make. A promise of harmony, a life lived at ease, Cottagecore's winter promise, a gentle winter breeze.

Amidst the tranquil haven of the Cottagecore lifestyle, synonymous with rural lifestyle, country living, slow living, or by whatever other name it is known for you, Winter casts its irresistible spell. Here, as the soft glow of hearth fires harmonizes with the graceful descent of snowflakes, I find myself unequivocally captivated by the enduring promise and allure that this cherished way of life holds.

It is a promise that extends far beyond the boundaries of a single season, transcending the confines of time and space to carve a place for itself in the very essence of everyday life. It beckons us to embrace a slower, more intentional way of living, one that finds solace in the rhythms of nature and celebrates the simple joys that each passing day brings.

The enduring spirit of Cottagecore whispers of a world where the bustling hum of modern life takes a back seat to the serenity of rustic simplicity and the beauty of mindful existence. It is a world where we learn to cherish the subtle nuances of the present moment,where we feel most alive, finding comfort in the familiar embrace of nature and the gentle symphony of the changing seasons. Through the lens of Cottagecore, we discover the profound beauty of a life lived in harmony with the earth, where the rich tapestry of natural wonders becomes a source of inspiration and a wellspring of gratitude.

These thoughts embraced me while watching "Emily of New Moon" by LM Montgomery, it brought a wave of nostalgia and a longing for simpler times. In that episode, although not directly about winter, it captures the magic of simple joys.

In Emily's town, as spring finally arrived, a collective joy seemed to bloom with the season. The community, weary of winter's confinement, welcomed the warmth and the chance to spend time outdoors. The air was filled with anticipation as Emily's school organized a trip to the beach—a rare and cherished event. Everyone prepared food and shared in the genuine happiness of the occasion.

This idyllic scene made me reflect on the stability and simplicity of life back then. The excitement of a beach trip with classmates was a highlight of the year. Winters were spent in the cozy company of loved ones and neighbors, creating bonds that sustained them through the cold months. With the arrival of spring, the promise of outdoor adventures with friends was enough to ignite a sense of wonder and delight.

In those days, the scarcity of options and the routine of simplicity made the most modest pleasures feel monumental. There was a rhythm to life that allowed people to savor each moment fully. The absence of constant distractions and endless choices meant that small events were deeply appreciated and held a special place in the heart. Today, we live in a world overflowing with possibilities and entertainment at our fingertips. Yet, this abundance often leads to a paradox of choice, where too many options result in a lack of true excitement. The constant availability of diversions can dull our sense of wonder and appreciation.

There's something profoundly lovely about the simplicity of yesteryears. The idea that a trip to the beach, a picnic, or the first bloom of spring could be the pinnacle of joy is a testament to the beauty of a stable, uncomplicated life. It's a reminder that sometimes, less truly is more. The fewer distractions we have, the more we can appreciate the simple, genuine moments that bring true happiness.

In reflecting on this, I find myself yearning for a return to that kind of simplicity, where every season brought its own unique pleasures, and where the joy of life was found in the little things. Perhaps my friend, by embracing a bit of that old-world simplicity, we can rekindle our ability to find profound happiness in the everyday wonders that surround us.

Yet, the promise of cottagecore is not one that is bound by the confines of a particular time of year. It is a guiding light that illuminates our path through the ever-shifting landscapes of spring, summer, autumn, and winter, infusing each passing day with a sense of wonder and appreciation. It encourages us to pause, to breathe, to feel alive with nature, and to immerse ourselves in the intricate details of the world around us, allowing us to revel in the magic that each season unfurls before our eyes.

From the vibrant blossoms of spring to the vibrant hues of fall, each moment becomes a canvas upon which the beauty of life is painted with exquisite detail.

Through the lens of Cottagecore, we learn to view every day as a precious gift, an opportunity to cultivate gratitude and find contentment in the small blessings. It is a reminder to embrace the present moment, to let go of the anxieties of the past and the uncertainties of the future, and to find joy in the here and now.

 In the pursuit of our long-term aspirations, it's all too easy to overlook the beauty of the present moment. Often, society encourages us to focus on distant career goals, academic achievements, or ambitious projects, with the promise that fulfillment lies at the end of this arduous journey. However, as we navigate this path, we may find ourselves becoming increasingly disconnected from the richness of life's everyday experiences. When our sole focus revolves around these far-off objectives, life can gradually transform into a monotonous and even burdensome existence. We risk losing ourselves in the relentless pursuit of success, at the expense of cherishing the fleeting moments that surround us.

It's essential to clarify that this perspective does not advocate for abandoning our careers or dismissing our studies. Instead, it encourages us to remember that life is not solely about the pursuit of distant goals, but also about finding joy and fulfillment in the present. It's about recognizing that the journey itself is just as meaningful as the destination. When we learn to strike a balance between our ambitions and our present experiences, we create a space for gratitude and contentment to flourish. We learn to celebrate each step forward, each milestone reached, and each lesson learned along the way.

While dedicating time and effort to our long-term objectives is crucial, it is equally important to cultivate an awareness of the beauty and richness that surrounds us on a daily basis. By embracing the unique lessons and blessings that each season of life brings, we infuse our journey with purpose and meaning. We learn to find joy not only in the destination but also in the process of getting there. Life becomes a tapestry woven with moments of growth, connection, and introspection, each contributing to the vibrant mosaic that makes up our existence.

Cottagecore, in all its rustic charm and tranquil allure, emerges as a gentle guiding light, leading us back to the foundational aspects of existence that truly matter. In the bustling rush of contemporary society, the simplicity of life's genuine pleasures often gets obscured by the demands of the fast-paced world. The soft crackle of a wood-burning fireplace, the shared warmth of a homemade meal, the joy of handcrafted creations, and the simple delight of gathering with loved ones encapsulate the heart and soul of Cottagecore living. Through this lens, we learn to cherish the intimate moments that shape our days, discovering solace in the profound beauty of life's unassuming blessings. It encourages us to step back from the relentless pursuit of material success and to delve into the richness of genuine connections and shared experiences.

Take, for instance, the joy of cultivating a modest garden patch, nurturing the growth of vibrant flowers and lush vegetables. The act of tending to the earth, witnessing the cycle of life firsthand, and relishing the fruits of one's labor instills a sense of purpose and accomplishment that transcends the trappings of modern success. As John Muir famously observed, "In every walk with nature, one receives far more than he seeks." Cottagecore embodies this sentiment, encouraging us to revel in the journey of learning, of immersing ourselves in new experiences, and finding joy in the process rather than solely fixating on the outcome.

 Moreover, Cottagecore celebrates the notion of shared moments and communal living, emphasizing the importance of forging deep connections with family and friends. It underscores the profound impact of laughter-filled conversations around a candlelit table, the comfort of storytelling by the fireside, and the bond of trust nurtured through genuine camaraderie. Ralph Waldo Emerson's words come to mind: "Nature always wears the colors of the spirit." The essence of Cottagecore again echoes this sentiment, reminding us that the heart of life's beauty lies not in the material possessions amassed, but in the immeasurable value of the memories etched in our hearts. In a world that often measures success through the lens of material accomplishments, Cottagecore remains a testament to the enduring legacy of a life well lived. It serves as a gentle reminder that our fulfillment stems not from the number of accolades amassed or the possessions acquired, but from the treasured moments shared with those who matter most. As the Cottagecore ethos continues to beckon us toward a simpler, more intentional way of living, it invites us to find contentment in the warmth of a shared meal, the laughter of dear friends, the embrace of a timeless tradition, and the beauty of life's subtle wonders.

This lifestyle nurtures an appreciation for the passage of time, for the ebb and flow of nature's rhythms, and for the seasonal transformations that bring a symphony of colors and scents. It encourages us to savor the crisp air of winter, the vibrant blooms of spring, the balmy days of summer, and the nostalgic rustle of autumn leaves. By tuning our senses to the subtle nuances of the changing seasons, we unlock a profound connection with the natural world, allowing us to witness the ever-evolving masterpiece of life that unfolds before us.

So, even as we bid adieu to the enchanting embrace of Cottagecore Winter, let us carry its timeless promise within our hearts, allowing it to guide us through the changing tides of time. May we continue to find solace and inspiration in the subtle wonders of the world around us, and may the spirit of Cottagecore serve as a gentle reminder that the truest joys in life are often found in the embrace of nature and the warmth of human connection.

Chapter VIII

Traditions and Tales

Weaving Winter's Stories

In the heart of the hearth, stories entwine, A tapestry of winter, tales so fine. With every crackling fire and shared delight, Traditions are woven, binding day to night.

From ancient folklore to the present's embrace, Winter's tales linger, weaving time and space. In each whispered anecdote and fond recollection, Traditions and tales find heartfelt connection.

Let's gather 'round the fire, with kin and friend, In the warmth of each story, let the heart mend. For in the weave of winter's tales, life finds its glory, Traditions forever etched, in memory's inventory.

Welcome, dear readers, to the captivating realm of "Traditions and Tales: Weaving Winter's Stories." Within the pages of this chapter, we embark on a spellbinding journey through the folklore, customs, and narratives that have woven themselves into the fabric of the winter season. Join me as we unravel the rich tapestry of cultural traditions that have stood the test of time, and immerse ourselves in the timeless tales that have kindled the warmth of community and companionship during the coldest months of the year.

From age-old customs to captivating legends, let us discover the enduring magic that resides within the heart of winter's stories. As we immerse ourselves in the enchanting world of winter folklore, customs, and narratives, we discover the timeless truths that transcend the boundaries of time and space, uniting us in a shared journey of understanding, empathy, and mutual respect. It is within the embrace of these enduring traditions that we find the enduring spirit of humanity, the echoes of our collective past, and the guiding light that illuminates the path to a more compassionate, connected, and harmonious future.

The enchanting tales of winter find their home through the frost-kissed air and the whispering pines, spinning a tapestry of wonder and mystique that transcends the confines of time. From the crackling flames of hearths to the hushed whispers of snowfall, the winter season makes us gather around the flickering light and share the age-old traditions and tales that have been passed down through generations.

The folklore, Customs, and Narratives

The folklore, customs, and narratives that have woven themselves into the fabric of the winter season are a rich tapestry of human history, cultural heritage, and the timeless wisdom that has guided communities through the ages. These enduring traditions carry the echoes of ancient civilizations and the collective experiences of generations, offering glimpses into the values, beliefs, and aspirations of societies past and present.

At the heart of these tales lie the cultural narratives that celebrate the winter solstice, a celestial event that marks the longest night of the year and the gradual return of the sun. Across various cultures, the solstice is embraced as a symbol of renewal and rebirth, a time to honor the cycles of nature and the promise of a brighter tomorrow. The rituals and customs associated with this pivotal moment vary widely, from the lighting of candles and the exchange of symbolic gifts to the performance of age-old ceremonies that seek to invoke the blessings of the divine.

In addition to the solstice celebrations, the folklore of winter often embraces mythical beings and fantastical creatures that personify the season's essence. From the frost-covered spirits that dance amidst the snowflakes to the benevolent guardians that watch over the land, these ethereal entities embody the enchantment and wonder that permeate the winter landscape. Their stories serve as cautionary tales, moral fables, and allegorical narratives that impart valuable lessons about courage, resilience, and the enduring power of the human spirit.

Whether it's the joyous festivities of Hanukkah, the vibrant revelry of Diwali, or the timeless celebrations of Christmas, these cultural observances underscore the importance of compassion, empathy, and the interconnectedness of humanity, the customs and traditions surrounding the winter season reflect a deep-seated reverence for community, togetherness, and the spirit of giving. They serve as a poignant reminder of the universal values that unite us all, transcending geographical boundaries and cultural differences to foster a sense of shared humanity and collective goodwill.

Embedded within the narratives of winter folklore are the ageless themes of hope, perseverance, and the resilience of the human spirit. They resonate with the echoes of the past, offering a glimpse into the collective consciousness of civilizations that have weathered the storms of history and emerged stronger, wiser, and more united. In their essence, these tales speak to the profound impact of storytelling as a vehicle for cultural preservation, communal bonding, and the transmission of knowledge from one generation to the next.

Celebrating The Winter Solstice

Celebrating the winter solstice is a time-honored tradition that has been observed by cultures around the world for centuries. It marks the shortest day and the longest night of the year, symbolizing the rebirth of light and the promise of new beginnings. As we honor this celestial event, we are invited to partake in various practices and rituals that pay homage to the natural rhythms of the universe and embrace the spirit of renewal and hope. Here are some ideas for you, dear readers, to celebrate the winter solstice and infuse this special occasion with meaning and joy:

Create a Solstice Altar: Craft a sacred space adorned with seasonal greenery, candles, and meaningful symbols that represent the essence of the winter solstice. Incorporate elements such as evergreen branches, pinecones, and crystals to evoke the spirit of nature and the enduring magic of the season.

Host a Feast of Abundance: Prepare a hearty feast featuring seasonal delights and bountiful harvest produce. Share in the joy of community and fellowship as you indulge in nourishing dishes that celebrate the gifts of the earth and the abundance of the season.

Perform a Ritual of Reflection: Take a moment for introspection and self-reflection, acknowledging the lessons and experiences of the past year. Light a candle in honor of your intentions and aspirations, setting forth your hopes and dreams for the year ahead with clarity and purpose.

Engage in Meditative Practices: Embrace the tranquility of the winter solstice by engaging in mindful activities such as yoga, meditation, or deep breathing exercises. Allow yourself to connect with the peaceful energy of the season, fostering a sense of inner balance and harmony.

Craft Sun-themed Decorations: Infuse your home with the radiance of the sun by creating handmade decorations inspired by its golden glow. Craft sun catchers, paper lanterns, or origami suns to adorn your living space, infusing it with warmth and vitality.

Share Stories and Legends: Gather around a cozy hearth or candlelit space and share stories and legends that honor the significance of the winter solstice. Delve into folklore and myths that highlight the triumph of light, wisdom, and the eternal cycle of nature's rhythms.

Offer Gratitude and Thanks: Take a moment to express gratitude for the blessings and abundance in your life. Whether through a heartfelt prayer, a gratitude journal, or a simple act of kindness, let gratitude be the guiding light that illuminates your path on this special day.

Stargazing and Moonlit Walks: Embrace the serene beauty of the winter night by indulging in stargazing or taking a moonlit walk under the celestial canopy. Revel in the tranquil stillness of the night and the awe-inspiring majesty of the cosmos above.

Plan for New Beginnings: Use the energy of the winter solstice to set intentions for the year ahead. Create a vision board, write down your aspirations, or embark on a creative project that reflects your dreams and goals, infusing your journey with purpose and inspiration.

As you celebrate the winter solstice, may you find solace in the embrace of nature's rhythms and the eternal dance of light and darkness. Embrace the spirit of renewal, the joy of community, and the promise of new beginnings as you welcome the return of the sun's radiant glow and the timeless magic of the season.

Winter Legends and Tales

Winter is a season rich with captivating legends and timeless tales that have been passed down through generations, each weaving a tapestry of wonder and enchantment. As we gather around the hearth or cozy up beneath blankets, let us immerse ourselves in these captivating stories that evoke the magic and mystery of the winter season. Here are some beloved winter legends and tales that you can share with your loved ones:

The Legend of Jack Frost

Delight in the whimsical tale of Jack Frost, the mischievous sprite who paints intricate frost patterns on windows and leaves delicate ice crystals in his wake. Follow his journey as he ushers in the frosty embrace of winter, bringing a touch of magic and wonder to the world.

The Snow Queen

Venture into the enchanting world of Hans Christian Andersen's "The Snow Queen," a timeless fairy tale that follows the adventures of Gerda and her quest to rescue her friend Kai from the clutches of the icy Snow Queen. Discover the enduring power of love and friendship as Gerda braves the wintry landscape to bring warmth and hope to a frozen heart.

The Wild Hunt

Uncover the haunting legend of the Wild Hunt, a spectral procession led by a mythical figure that roams the winter night skies. Listen to the tales of ancient folklore that speak of ghostly huntsmen and their spectral hounds as they traverse the wintry landscape, their howls echoing through the frost-laden forests.

The Legend of the Ice Maiden

Immerse yourself in the legend of the Ice Maiden, a fabled enchantress who weaves intricate snowflakes and commands the icy winds of winter. Discover her story of mystery and magic, as she bestows her blessings upon those who honor the beauty and serenity of the winter season.

The Yule Cat

Delve into Icelandic folklore and the legend of the Yule Cat, a formidable feline said to roam the snowy countryside during the winter solstice. Listen to the tales of this mystical cat, who is believed to bring good fortune to those who receive new clothing as gifts, and misfortune to those who remain without.

The Tale of the Nutcracker

Immerse yourself in the classic tale of "The Nutcracker," a heartwarming story that unfolds on a magical Christmas Eve. Follow the journey of Clara and her beloved Nutcracker as they venture into the Land of Sweets, encountering a cast of whimsical characters and experiencing the joy of the holiday season.

The Legend of Boreas

Explore the ancient Greek legend of Boreas, the god of the cold north wind, who ushers in the frigid embrace of winter. Unravel the myths that surround this legendary figure, known for his fierce temperament and the wintry storms that he brings in his wake.

The Winter's Night

Dive into the folklore of different cultures that celebrate the mystical allure of the winter's night. Listen to stories of celestial beings, twinkling stars, and shimmering constellations that illuminate the wintry skies, casting a spell of wonder and awe over the world below.

As you share these winter legends and tales with your loved ones, may you find yourself enveloped in the timeless magic of storytelling, where the boundaries between reality and imagination blur, and the spirit of the season comes alive in every word and every moment shared.

"The Winter Visitor"

Amidst the biting chill of winter, a small town nestled in the mountains found itself bracing for the harsh season ahead. The residents had grown accustomed to the bitter winds and the frost-covered landscape, but this winter was different. As the snow piled high, and the icy gusts grew stronger, a sense of despair loomed over the once cheerful community.

It was on the coldest night of the year that the townsfolk experienced a peculiar occurrence. A mysterious figure, draped in a cloak of warmth, appeared on the outskirts of the town. No one knew where the stranger had come from, but as the word spread of their arrival, a flicker of hope ignited in the hearts of the freezing residents.

The stranger moved with an air of grace and purpose, their presence seemingly thawing the frost that had settled in the hearts of the townspeople. With gentle gestures and a kind smile, they began to distribute bundles of firewood, blankets, and hot meals, providing solace to those in need.

As the days passed, the stranger continued to weave their magic, bringing comfort and joy to every doorstep. Their acts of kindness inspired the community to band together, to share what little they had, and to create a warmth that surpassed the bitter bite of winter.

Whispers soon circulated that the mysterious figure was the embodiment of the season's spirit, a visitor sent to remind the townsfolk of the power of unity and compassion. Though their origins remained a mystery, their impact on the town was undeniable. With the stranger's guidance, the community not only weathered the harsh winter but also emerged stronger and more united than ever before.

The legend of the Winter Visitor persisted for generations, a cherished tale passed down from parents to children, a reminder that even in the darkest of times, the warmth of the human spirit can illuminate the coldest of winters.

Chapter IX

What Winter Teaches Us

Life Lessons

*In the gentle hush of winter, nature's pace reveals,
Life's lesson in slowing, its rhythm gently appeals.
From the stillness of snowfall to the patience of
ice, Winter whispers softly, teaching us to be wise.*

*With every snowflake's descent, a call to pause,
To embrace the quiet, to live without cause. In the
dormant landscapes, a lesson in rest, What winter
teaches us, is to be at our best.*

*Let's heed its gentle guidance, as nature's own
disciple, For in the art of slowing, we find life's
true stifle. In winter's patient teachings, may our
souls ignite, To live like the seasons, embracing
stillness in flight.*

Let us now dear friends, open our hearts to the profound teachings that this enchanting season has to offer. In this chapter, we delve into the wisdom and life lessons that winter bestows upon us, transcending its chilly exterior to reveal the invaluable insights and experiences that shape our understanding of the world. Let us uncover the depths of meaning and inspiration hidden within the wintry landscape, allowing its quiet serenity and transformative power to guide us on a path of self-discovery and growth.

We will explore how mindfulness is illuminated through the lens of winter and the practices we can glean from this introspective season. Winter's invitation to delve inward becomes a catalyst for fostering self-care, introspection, and intentional living. From cultivating mindfulness in our daily routines to nurturing our emotional well-being, the lessons that winter imparts resonate deeply with the essence of mindful living. As the world outside quiets down, we are prompted to embark on a journey of self-discovery, to tend to the garden of our souls, and to nurture the seeds of inner peace and serenity. Get cozy and let us delve into the practices that allow us to embody the spirit of winter and infuse our lives with the richness of mindful awareness.

It is through these facets of the winter season that we uncover the profound teachings that shape our perspectives and inform our journeys. As we traverse the frost-laden paths and bask in the glow of hearth fires, may we heed the lessons that winter whispers to us, allowing them to kindle a sense of wisdom and resilience within our hearts. Let us embrace the transformative power of this season and emerge with a renewed appreciation for the intricate tapestry of life that unfolds before us.

Embracing Stillness

In the hush of winter's embrace, we learn the art of stillness. Nature's quietude envelops us, urging us to find solace in moments of peaceful reflection. As the world outside slows down, we too are invited to pause and connect with the tranquility that resides within. The barren trees and the soft blanket of snow remind us that growth often emerges from the depths of stillness. In the words of John Burroughs, "The lesson which life repeats and constantly enforces is 'look under foot.' You are always nearer to the divine and the true sources of your power than you think."

Finding Beauty in Simplicity

Winter's stark landscape beckons us to find beauty in the simplicity that surrounds us. The delicate intricacies of snowflakes, the gentle curve of a frozen stream, and the ethereal glow of moonlit snow inspire us to see the world through a lens of wonder and appreciation. In the words of Albert Camus, "In the depth of winter, I finally learned that within me there lay an invincible summer."

Resilience in Adversity

The harsh winds and biting cold of winter embody the resilience needed to endure adversity. The enduring strength of nature's elements mirrors the fortitude within us, encouraging us to weather life's storms with courage and grace. Winter's icy grip, while formidable, eventually gives way to the tender buds of spring, reminding us of the ebb and flow of life's challenges. As Haruki Murakami said, "And once the storm is over, you won't remember how you made it through, how you managed to survive. You won't even be sure whether the storm is really over. But one thing is certain. When you come out of the storm, you won't be the same person who walked in."

Appreciating Transience and Impermanence

Winter's transience whispers to us the fragility of life and the impermanence of all things. The fleeting beauty of frost-kissed mornings and the ephemeral magic of snowfall teach us to cherish each passing moment, for nothing lasts forever. The barren trees that once flourished serve as a poignant reminder of the cyclical nature of existence and the inevitability of change. In the words of Rumi, "The quieter you become, the more you can hear."

Cultivating Respite and Renewal

Amidst winter's frosty grip, we learn the importance of seeking respite and renewal. The longer nights and shorter days offer an opportunity for introspection and self-care, encouraging us to nurture our inner landscapes and tend to the gardens of our souls. Winter's respite becomes a sanctuary where we can recharge and emerge with newfound vigor, ready to embrace the blooming possibilities of the seasons to come. As Anne Bradstreet once mused, "If we had no winter, the spring would not be so pleasant: if we did not sometimes taste of adversity, prosperity would not be so welcome."

Gratitude for Warmth and Comfort

Winter's biting chill heightens our gratitude for the warmth and comfort that envelop us. The crackling hearth and the cozy embrace of blankets remind us of the simple joys of life and the blessings that often go unnoticed. The contrast between the frosty landscape and the hearth's tender glow ignites a profound appreciation for the comfort and security that nurture our spirits during the coldest of days. As Marcel Proust once eloquently stated, "Let us be grateful to people who make us happy; they are the charming gardeners who make our souls blossom."

Reveling in Individuality and Uniqueness

In the intricate patterns of each snowflake lies a reminder of the individuality that exists within the unity of nature. No two snowflakes are alike, each crafted with precision and care, and yet, as they come together to form a soft, white blanket over the land, they create a unified spectacle of unparalleled beauty. It is as though nature is whispering to us, urging us to recognize the beauty that lies within our own uniqueness and the strength that can be found in unity. The snowflakes' dance in the wintry air becomes a metaphor for life itself, a reminder that even in the face of adversity and change, there exists a quiet beauty that can unite us all in a shared journey through the seasons of life.

Nurturing Introspection and Self-Discovery

Winter's introspective aura invites us to embark on a journey of self-discovery. The longer nights and contemplative atmosphere provide an ideal backdrop for delving into the depths of our souls and uncovering the hidden truths that define us. As we navigate the quietude of winter, we find solace in self-reflection and introspection, nurturing a deeper understanding of our desires, fears, and aspirations. In the words of Carl Jung, "Your vision will become clear only when you look into your heart. Who looks outside, dreams; who looks inside, awakes."

May these timeless lessons of winter guide us through the seasons of life, imparting wisdom, resilience, and a deeper appreciation for the profound mysteries that unfold before us. As we embrace the teachings that winter bestows, may we find ourselves enriched by its power and inspired to greet each day with newfound grace and understanding.

SELF-CARE PRACTICES FOR WINTER

Winter self-care is essential for maintaining well-being during the colder months when the harsh weather can often take a toll on both our physical and mental health. It's a time to be gentle with ourselves, to prioritize rest and relaxation, and to indulge in activities that bring us comfort and joy. Taking care of our bodies, minds, and spirits becomes crucial during this season, allowing us to thrive despite the challenges that winter may present.

Here are some tips for winter self-care to help you navigate the season with a sense of balance and well-being:

Warm Baths and Aromatherapy: Take indulgent warm baths infused with essential oils like lavender or eucalyptus to soothe your senses and relax your body. Let the warm water envelop you, providing a comforting escape from the chilly weather outside.

Moisturizing Skincare Routine: Adjust your skincare routine to include richer, more hydrating products to combat the dryness that often accompanies winter. Use nourishing moisturizers, hydrating serums, and gentle exfoliants to keep your skin healthy and glowing despite the cold, harsh air.

Cozy Reading Time: Set aside dedicated time for cozy reading sessions, wrapped in soft blankets with a steaming cup of tea or hot chocolate by your side. Allow yourself to escape into the pages of a good book, embracing the serenity and comfort that reading provides.

Mindful Meditation and Yoga: Incorporate mindfulness practices and gentle yoga into your daily routine to center yourself and find inner peace. Cultivate a sense of calm and balance through deep breathing exercises and gentle stretching, allowing yourself to let go of stress and tension.

Winter Walks in Nature: Despite the cold, take time to go for brisk walks in the crisp winter air. Bundle up in warm clothing and immerse yourself in the beauty of the winter landscape. The fresh air and natural surroundings can invigorate your senses and lift your spirits.

Comfort Food Cooking: Experiment with cooking hearty, nourishing meals that bring warmth and comfort to your body and soul. Prepare soups, stews, and roasted vegetables using seasonal ingredients to create satisfying and wholesome dishes that embrace the flavors of winter.

Creative Indoor Hobbies: Engage in creative indoor hobbies such as painting, knitting, or crafting to stimulate your mind and channel your emotions into artistic expression. Allow yourself the freedom to explore your creative instincts and enjoy the process of bringing your ideas to life.

Candlelit Evenings and Relaxation: Create a cozy atmosphere at home with the soft, flickering light of candles. Settle into moments of relaxation and reflection, allowing the gentle ambiance to calm your mind and promote a sense of tranquility and inner peace.

Nourish Your Body: Enjoy nourishing, hearty meals that provide your body with the nutrients it needs during the colder months. Incorporate seasonal fruits and vegetables, whole grains, and immune-boosting foods to support your overall health and well-being.

Stay Active: Engage in regular physical activity to boost your energy levels and enhance your mood. Whether it's indoor workouts, yoga sessions, or brisk winter walks, staying active can help combat the lethargy often associated with the winter season.

By adding these winter-time self-care practices into your daily routine, you can foster a sense of well-being and balance, allowing yourself to thrive during the colder months and emerge with a rejuvenated spirit as spring approaches.

Chapter X

Finding Your Way

Winter Index

In the tapestry of winter, each story intertwines, A symphony of unique journeys, where every spirit shines. With every entry and every heartfelt line, The winter index unites, where differences align.

From snow-capped peaks to the valley's embrace, The index reveals how each person finds their place. In the diversity of experiences, nature's threads are spun, Binding us together in the season's hum.

Let's cherish its diversity, as each tale takes flight, For in the winter index, we find a common light. In its carefully curated pages, may our hearts unite, To celebrate our shared winter, in its purest delight.

Dear Kindred spirits,

I think That this is the most important chapter in this book! Allow me to offer you a word of gentle guidance. While I want *"The Cottagecore Winter"* to serve as a wellspring of inspiration, let us not forget that life is **not a meticulously planned script**. Rather, it is a magnificent tapestry woven with the threads of unpredictability and spontaneity. As you peruse the anecdotes and musings shared here, remember that the true magic of existence lies not in adhering strictly to a checklist but in finding joy in the unscripted moments, in surrendering to the unpredictable cadence of life.

Let us approach each entry in this narrative as an opportunity to invite the enchantment of the season into our lives, yet also as a reminder that life's most poignant moments often arise unexpectedly, in the laughter that echoes in the crisp winter air, in the spontaneous strolls through snow-laden woods, and in the warmth of impromptu gatherings with cherished company. It is in these unassuming yet profound instances that we find the true essence of a fulfilling life. So, let us use these offerings as a compass, guiding us toward a deeper connection with the essence of winter, and let us cherish the magic that unfolds when we allow life to happen, unencumbered by plans and schedules. Embracing the enchantment of winter isn't confined to a set of rules or obligations; it's a journey unique to each individual, filled with the magic of the unexpected.

So my friend, let us release any pressures of conforming to a predefined winter script. There's no need to rush into purchasing elaborate decorations or transforming your space if it doesn't resonate with you. The essence of winter can effortlessly infuse your daily life, subtly weaving its way through the delicate snowfall and the quiet beauty of a frost-covered morning.

Our winter bucket lists are not meant to be strict schedules to adhere to; they are simply whispers of inspiration, guiding us toward experiences that might spark joy or ignite our curiosity. These lists are gentle reminders of the countless possibilities that winter presents, encouraging us to step outside our comfort zones and discover the magic hidden within the frost-kissed days. Whether it's a solitary walk in a snow-covered forest, a spontaneous sledding adventure with friends, or a cozy night spent reading by the fire, let these activities be invitations to create cherished memories, not burdensome tasks to be checked off.

In the gentle ebb and flow of the season, let's remember to embrace the unplanned moments, the unexpected detours, and the delightful surprises that life often presents. These are the threads that weave the rich tapestry of our existence, adding depth and meaning to our everyday lives. Let us honor the serendipitous beauty of life, where the most profound joy often arises from the simplest, unscripted moments. For in the quiet simplicity of a winter's day, amidst the soft crunch of snow underfoot and the soothing crackle of a warm hearth, we discover that the true essence of happiness lies in embracing life as it comes, with an open heart and a willing spirit.

In the age of constant connectivity and digital immersion, our minds are often bombarded with carefully curated images of lavish decorations, picturesque winter retreats, and seemingly idyllic lifestyles that seem to adorn the screens of our social media feeds. Leaving us with a sense of inadequacy and a nagging feeling that our own lives fall short, this can sow seeds of discontent within us, leading us to believe that our own experiences pale in comparison to the glossy narratives that dominate our screens. We find ourselves falling prey to the pressure to keep up with the latest trends, to meticulously decorate our homes to match the images we see online, and to follow suit with a never-ending list of winter activities that seem to be the hallmark of a fulfilling winter experience.

However, even if we do those activities, the reality often falls short of these lofty expectations, leaving us feeling disillusioned and disconnected from the true essence of the season. Instead of finding joy in the simple pleasures that winter offers, we become fixated on chasing an ideal that is inherently unattainable. It is in these moments that we must remind ourselves of the importance of taking a step back, of reevaluating our relationship with social media, and of embracing the concept of mindful consumption.

By indulging in periodic social media detoxes and limiting our intake of curated content, we afford ourselves the opportunity to recalibrate our perspectives and see what really matters to us, to realign our focus with the richness of the present moment. We come to recognize that each life is inherently unique and special in its own way, and that comparison is a futile exercise that happens subconsciously that only serves to diminish the value of our own experiences. When we create space for introspection and self-discovery, we open ourselves up to a world of wonder and appreciation for the moments that make our own lives extraordinary.

 Limiting our content intake serves as a powerful antidote to the anxieties and inadequacies that can be fueled by endless scrolling. By immersing ourselves in the tactile, sensory experiences of the season, we are reminded that true fulfillment doesn't stem from conforming to the idealized standards set by the digital world, but from cherishing the fleeting moments that are uniquely ours.

Let us not allow the pressures of social media and societal expectations to diminish the magic of our own personal journey. Instead, let us choose to revel in the beauty of the everyday, to cherish the warmth of our own hearths, and to find solace in the unassuming yet profound moments that define our winter experiences. As we cultivate a sense of mindfulness and gratitude, may we find fulfillment not in the pursuit of external validation, but in the quiet joy of embracing the genuine, unfiltered realities that make our lives uniquely beautiful.

In our quest for fulfillment, it's essential to pause and recalibrate, allowing gratitude to seep into our lives. By appreciating the everyday beauty of winter — from the gentle sway of bare branches to the soft warmth of a cozy blanket — we rekindle our sense of contentment. We find comfort in knowing that our existence, marked by the ebb and flow of ordinary moments, holds the potential for fulfillment in its own right.

Kindred spirit, I encourage you to consider taking a step back from the overwhelming digital realm, even if it's just for a brief respite. Whether it's a week-long social media detox, a three-day hiatus, or even a single day dedicated to mindful disconnection, the act of consciously moderating your exposure to online content can be remarkably rejuvenating. It's about finding a starting point that feels right for you, an entryway into a world of heightened awareness and a reconnection with the simple, often overlooked joys that surround us.

CONCLUSION

Farewell, dear winter, with your frost-kissed morn,
Your whispered tales and the grace you have borne.
In your icy embrace, we found solace and light,
Now, as you depart, you leave us in delight.

From snow-laden pathways to the cozy hearth's
glow, You've painted a canvas with your serene,
tranquil flow. Though you now fade, your
memories will endure, In the hearts you've touched,
steadfast and sure.

So, farewell, dear winter, as you take your leave,
Your enchanting spirit in our minds we'll weave.
Till next we meet, in your snowy embrace,
Farewell, dear winter, with your quiet, gentle
grace.

As we draw the curtains on this immersive journey through the ethereal wonderland of *"The Cottagecore Winter"*, it's with a heart brimming with nostalgia and gratitude that I reflect upon the moments we've shared together. From the captivating whispers of snow to the alluring aromas of simmering stews and spiced beverages, we've unearthed the profound richness of this enchanting season. We've unraveled the threads of nature's tapestry, finding solace in the simplicity of a snow-covered landscape and the gentle crackle of a comforting hearth. The beauty of winter lies not just in its visual splendor but in the way it beckons us to slow down and savor the often overlooked treasures nestled within its frosty embrace.

Through our collective journey, we've delved into the essence of slow living, discovering the profound joy that can be found in the unhurried rhythm of everyday life. We've celebrated the art of being present, basking in the quiet moments that winter so generously bestows upon us. As we bid adieu, remember to carry with you the spirit of winter's serenity, allowing it to infuse each passing day with a sense of wonder and gratitude.

May the lessons gleaned from this exploration inspire you to nurture a deeper connection with the natural world and to relish the enchantment that resides within the seemingly mundane.

As I poured my heart and passion into the pages of this book "The Cottagecore Winter", I envisioned it as a gentle lantern, illuminating the path for those who seek to rekindle the warmth of connection and joy during the winter months.

I hope I have succeeded in inspiring you and sprinkling a little joy into your heart. If my words have resonated with you, I would love to hear your good thoughts and reflections. Your encouraging feedback is invaluable to me, dear reader, and it would mean the world if you could share your good reviews on platforms like Amazon and Goodreads. Your thoughts serve as a beacon, guiding kindred spirits to discover the enchantment nestled within these pages. Together, let's amplify the beauty of this journey, ensuring that more hearts can find solace and inspiration in the essence of cottagecore.

THE END

Made in the USA
Las Vegas, NV
26 November 2024

12678625R00076